I love my daddy. He h
me. I love this book as it speaks so intimately of how God's love works in
the most difficult moments in our lives. As Christians, I believe that we
will all dance with our Father one day.

Sandi Patty
Christian artist and 40-time Dove Award winner

I thank God that I do not fully understand what it feels like to lose a child.
That is something reserved, I imagine, only for those who have been forced
to endure the most unthinkable tragedy any parent could suffer.

In this book, however, I am able to feel both Randy's pain at the loss of his
precious daughter, but also the joy that remains in so many loving memories
of her that will live on in his heart until the day that they are together again.
This is a story with the power to help comfort and guide those who seek
solace in the midst of the unthinkable.

Dan Dean,
Senior Pastor, Heartland Church, Carrollton, Texas
Lead Singer, Phillips, Craig and Dean

There are so many lessons to be learned in this poignant recounting of a
daughter's short life through the eyes of her father. Randy beautifully tells
the story of his brave little girl Jennie's 26 year battle with cancer. Seizing
life, leaving nothing unsaid, believing that God is ultimately good in all
things . . . there are countless take-aways. This book with make you laugh
and surely cry, but above all it will make you think about your own life,
and how you can better live it to God's glory.

Shelley Breen, Point of Grace

One of the elements of this book I enjoyed was Randy's use of great narraphors (a new word I coined combining "narrative" and "metaphors") in the "Bridges" section of the book. The word pictures help tell the story in a very compelling way.

Dr. Leonard Sweet
Author, E. Stanley Jones Professor of Evangelism at Drew University

Henri Nouwen writes about "befriending death" before you die, which makes your spirit accessible to those you leave behind. If there's anyone who has befriended death with a smile and a dance, it is Jennie. What faith and courage she embodied, especially during the Talk, and her last dance with her father,

Michael J. Christensen, Ph.D.
Director, Communities of Shalom
Drew University

Conversations
with an
Angel

Dr. Randy Schuneman DMin, DAd

WESTBOW
PRESS

A DIVISION OF THOMAS NELSON

Unless otherwise indicated, all scripture quotations are from
The Holy Bible, New International Version.

Cover photos by the author.

Visit www.JennieShoe.com for discussions, more chapters, and free PDF versions of this book which can be shared freely. Also, follow Randy Schuneman at Twitter @RandySchuneman and on Facebook at facebook.com/rschuneman.

WestBow Press books may be ordered through booksellers or by contacting:

WestBow Press
A Division of Thomas Nelson
1663 Liberty Drive
Bloomington, IN 47403
www.westbowpress.com
1-(866) 928-1240

ISBN: 978-1-4497-3876-1 (sc)
ISBN: 978-1-4497-3875-4 (hc)
ISBN: 978-1-4497-3877-8 (e)

Library of Congress Control Number: 2012901620

Printed in the United States of America

WestBow Press rev. date: 02/07/2012

Contents

Foreword.. xiii

Introduction..xv

Part One: Life And Death

In The Beginning
My Partner in Time...1
I Should Have Known She Was an Angel 5
My Eyes Adored Her! 10
Bubba 12
The Mischief Makers Club 16

Reigning Cats And Dogs
Love Me, Love My Pet 21
Here Kitty, Kitty! 22
All Dogs Go To Heaven 25
Sorry, Charlie! 29

Bad Cell Connections
You Are One in Three Million...35
Dr. Doom 39
Not Again 42
School Daze 44
Hair Today . . . Gone Tomorrow 47
Oh, My God! 49
Night Moves 52
I Am Just Guessing...55

Nurse Jennie
All My Children...61
76 Trombones Led the Big Parade 64

Stoop-ing to New Heights..67
Don't PICC on Me...70
Bottoms Up! 73

Room 591
8 Day Week 77
When God's Silence is Deafening...................................82
The Talk..88
Red-Toed Elephants and Pink Fingernails 93
Show Me the Money! 96
That Goes in the Book 100
Let's Party..106
The Last Dance 109

Going Home
Houston, We Have a Problem! 115
Someone Call Security!...117
Angels of Mercy 120
The Day Jennie Died..122

Part Two: Grief

God's Pre-Emptive Strike
A Deeper Kind of Grace..139
The Return of the Waltons 140
Angelic Visitations 146
I Just Can't Do This!...151

The Firsts
The First Time Ever I Saw 155
I've Fallen and I Can't Get Up! 156
Letting the Cat Out of the Bag......................................161
The First Noel 164
A Day of Remembrance 167
Was it a Morning Like This 170
The Last First 175

Bridges Over Troubled Water
In Grave Condition...181
Special Agent 007...183
The Bridge of Numbness..187

The Bridge of Anger 190
The Bridge of the Perfect Storm 195
The Bridge of Waves..198
The Bridge of Brokenness...200

Appendix

Shock and Awe..207
God is Good . . . All the Time..210
Standing Stone..213
Sunflower Seeds are Good For your Memory 216
A Broken Heart Still Beats..219
The Epilogue...222
Jennie's Obituary..225

Acknowledgments 229

This book is dedicated to:

My wife Bonnie who has walked with me for 39 years as we journeyed through each story you will read. She is God's perfect choice to be the mother of an angel.

My son Robb, who is my cheerleader, my adviser and the epitome of what it means to be a brother.

And, of course, to the angel that God loaned our family for thirty-two years: my daughter Jennifer who taught me more about life, courage and faith in God than I could ever have taught her.

Do not forget to entertain strangers, for by so doing some people have entertained angels without knowing it.
Hebrews 13:2

Foreword

If Randy Schuneman ever intended to be an author, he never mentioned it. I still remember the day we met. It was a Sunday morning in Flint, Michigan and neither of us could have anticipated how our stories would intertwine in the years ahead. In fact, in the nearly two decades since, we have analyzed everything from baseball to theology (in that order), and not one time—through all the meals, the rounds of golf, the phone calls—did he ever say anything about a book. It was never in the plan. After all, we were both called to ministry, but by completely different roads. He was the pastor and I was the writer. He was comfortable in the pulpit in much the same way I was with a pencil and legal pad.

So what changed? I think he would probably tell you *everything did*. It wasn't all at once or even over a year or two, but almost as if one word at a time, the story was pursuing the author. Conversations about Beanie Babies and baby dolls evolved into talks about cancer and chemo and hospice and—long before the writer was ready—in death, the story found life.

What every storyteller (even the unintended ones) eventually learn is that life's encounters should not, nor cannot be silenced. The theology of the writer believes God will never waste the narrative of pain. Comfort is found in the knowledge that when the pen becomes too heavy to bear, God comes along side and gathers up all the words and puts them in the proper order on just the right pages.

And so . . . the one who never intended to be an author invites us into the story. Withholding nothing, he writes about the Jennie I knew and loved and a family's grief of letting go. My prayer for you the reader is that you will rediscover within these pages the story of God's grace. After all, the story was never ours to begin with. Sometimes He just lets us be the one to tell it.

- Dave Clark, *October 2011*

Introduction

On June 17, 2010, my family and I entered a darker dimension of life than I ever knew existed. On that day, we began a journey that no one would choose for themselves. On that Thursday in June, my daughter died.

After two and a half months of struggling with advanced liver cancer, Jennifer Dawn Schuneman passed away and our lives were forever changed. Her death left a huge hole in our hearts.

It will never be completely filled until we embrace her again in heaven.

I've been given books about the grieving process, written by people who had experienced the loss of a loved one. I often found this discouraging, because most of those books were written many years after the death occurred. The pain experienced immediately after that loss, though, is radically different than even two years later. In either case, the world will never be the same again, but it becomes easier to talk about death in an objective manner as time passes. The tears still come, but not as often. When we mention their names, we begin to smile again as we remember their stories imprinted on our hearts. Our emotions are not as raw as they once were.

In talking to friends who lost family members, I found myself asking one question: "How do you get through this?" The most common answer I received was, "It just takes time." It is somewhat true that time will help in the healing process. However, at the beginning of the journey of grieving, "time" feels synonymous with "forever." Everyone is seeking a quick fix for overcoming the heartache that consumes them, but even God feels a million miles away.

I truly felt called to write this book. If I had chosen the best person from my family to write it, I would have been my fourth choice (out of four). My first choice would have been my daughter Jennifer. She would have been able to tell you exactly what she was feeling as she experienced her life. She could have described the inner emotions of a person who is dying. Jennie would have written this whole book in poetic form. She could have told you about her life and made it all rhyme. Among other things, Jennie was a poet. She could write the silliest rhymes or the most deeply meaningful words from her heart. Plus if she had written this book, it would mean she was still here with us.

There is a tie for my second choice. I would have chosen Bonnie, because no one was closer to Jennie than my wife. There have been few loves that went so deep. She could tell of the emotions that a mother and daughter have and the ties between them. I think she would also challenge every woman to find peace with their mother or daughter. What Bonnie would not give to have another day with Jennie.

I would also choose Bonnie because she taught me to write in a way that came alive. When Bonnie and I were working together at West Flint Church of the Nazarene in Flint, Michigan, I would write a monthly article for the newsletter. I submitted it to Bonnie so she could print it. I quickly began to notice that what I wrote and what was printed were not even close to the same. The printed words jumped off the page! My words, on the other hand, lay still like a sleeping ferret.

When I finally raised the issue, Bonnie told me something I have never forgotten, "If you are not involved in what you are writing, why would anyone want to read it? You have to keep people asking, "What happens next? Why should I be interested in what I am reading? If you are not interesting, why should we be interested?"

Bonnie, I want to thank you for teaching me to write with passion. It prepared me for this journey. We shared a passion for the focus of this book five years before she was born. I am sorry if my questions about details ever caused you any pain. I just wanted to tell Jennie's story accurately.

Tied for my second choice would be my son Robbie. I would choose Robbie, because he is a far better writer than I am. He could write about buttering toast and make it interesting. He can be deeper than anyone I have ever known, then as funny as you will find. Robb wrote his sister's obituary. It was a masterpiece! Robb is a gifted writer. You would have enjoyed his book about his sister more than what I present to you. Robb could have told Jennie's story from a sibling's perspective. Jennie and Robbie had a wonderful relationship. There are things that Jennie knew about Robbie long before I ever found out. Robb could speak to Jennie during her illness at times when I was not emotionally able to say a word.

Robb would have been a perfect choice to write this book, because he showed strength and courage that made impossible circumstances possible. Robb, I need you to know that we never would have made it through those ten hellish weeks without you! I have loved you throughout your life, but you showed a depth of character during Jennie's illness and death that I wish I had. Thanks for being there when, emotionally, I could not do anything. You have been my confidante since you were little. Your wisdom amazes me; I hate to admit it, but you are usually right.

In spite of my ranking, God chose me to tell Jennie's story. I realize that fathers are supposed to teach their children about life. In my case, I learned more about God from the face of an angel named Jennie than I ever did in College and Seminary. Our conversations over her 32 years taught me about faith in Christ and about God's grace, forgiveness, mercy and love.

If I have a writing gift, it is that I put my heart on paper. You will not find this book to be the most eloquent ever written. If you looking for a theological treatise on the Christian perspective of death, keep looking! If you are looking for a dissertation filled with footnotes and citations, this is not the book for you. Imagine sitting down with a cup of coffee or a soft drink and talking about life. That's what this book is about.

After fifteen months, my emotions are still raw. My journey is different than yours. I cannot tell you that I "understand how you feel." What I can tell you is that you are not alone. You would be amazed to know how many people are on this journey with you.

The other truth I need to share is, "You will make it!" On those dark days when things seem so bleak, hang on to that truth. Do not let the clouds of the present block your vision for the future. Even though the past will haunt you at times, just know it will also become a trusted friend and a source of joy.

Although I pastored for 33 years, I am not writing this book as a pastor. Although I have a doctorate, I am not trying to impress you with my knowledge. There is so much that I do not understand about this whole journey. I am writing this story as a brokenhearted Dad whose whole life has been changed by God, who loved us enough to send our family an angel named Jennie.

Jennie's birth, childhood cancer, life, calling—and death—have changed the person that I am. In the midst of all the joy and sorrow, I have been molded into the person that I am today. I will be honest— being like Jesus hurts sometimes. I never fully understood what it meant to be "conformed into His likeness" (Romans 8:29) until I experienced

His hand at work through the experiences of the past year and three months.

If I have done what I set out to do, you will feel this book. Be forewarned: you may cry at several points in this journey. You will also laugh! Those are the emotions of life. Most of these pages are "tear-stained." At times, I cried so hard that I could not see the computer screen. At other times, I had to wipe away tears from laughter. A well-lived life should evoke both emotions. Jennie's life certainly did.

The book came together in such a way that each chapter stands on its own, so I have decided to make all of these chapters downloadable, for free, from my website at *www.JennieShoe. com*. This book is a "living book." If I tried to put all of my love for Jennie between two covers, it would make *War and Peace* look like a first-grade primer. This means I will also continue to write new chapters and put them online at the same website. I want to start a conversation between us about how we are dealing with our grief. You can find more information about that in the appendix.

And if you get tired of me along the way, I've put poems that Jennie wrote on the title pages throughout this book. They are delightful memories of Jennie. I hope you like them as much as I do.

This book was written for two audiences: those who are grieving and those who aren't. For those who are experiencing grief, hopefully there will be encouragement and tools that will help you. For those who are not, hopefully you find tips on what to do, and what to avoid, when you are dealing with someone else's loss. And hopefully you will also meet my daughter, Jennifer Dawn Schuneman. I think you'll find her to be an amazing young woman. What an angel!

Part One:
Life And Death

In The Beginning

My Partner in Time

BONNIE SUE MULLINS was born on September 30 in the same year I was. She arrived at Ponca City Memorial Hospital in Ponca City, Oklahoma. She was the fourth child born to Jennie Bernice (Isaacs) and Harold Mullins. Bonnie hails from the Mullins Ranch, located almost halfway between Ponca City, Oklahoma and Stillwater, Oklahoma.

Because Bonnie, like me, was raised in a wonderful Christian home, preparation was a vital key to being ready for church and church activities. The Mullins family went to Sunday morning, Sunday evening and Wednesday evening services every week. They attended all Revival Services plus any teen activities and other church gatherings. They were an "every-time-the-church's-doors-are-open" family whose faithfulness could be counted on like clockwork. The family car left for church at exactly 8:30 a.m. on Sunday morning. If the women were not ready on time, Harold would begin honking the car horn. Three women trying to get ready with one bathroom made schedules tight quite often. Frustrated, Bonnie and her mom came out in their slips one morning to make their point. The honking continued.

Bonnie learned a good work ethic on the farm. There were always meals to prepare for the workers, especially at harvest. There were chores to be done, like cleaning the house or washing dishes. She learned to not stop until the job was completed. Bonnie's dad taught her how to deal creatively with problems (baling wire is a farmer's duct tape, for instance). Bonnie's mom taught her how to be prim and proper. Immodesty would not be tolerated.

Jennie got her love for music and animals from Bonnie. Both my girls loved to play piano and sing. Music was a part of Bonnie and Jennie's DNA. Jennie's love for animals came naturally as well. While Bonnie had coyotes, snakes and frogs, Jennie had parakeets, goldfish and newts.

I first met Bonnie when we were 16. Our families go further back than that, but I really got to know her while we served on a teen singing group called "The Northwest Oklahoma District Impact Team." We practiced a few times a year and then went out to do work projects at nearby churches. Our biggest gig was a one-time performance at Bethany First Church of the Nazarene. The crowd that day was bigger than my hometown.

I liked Bonnie, but was really immature in the ways that I showed it. When we were at a large teen gathering called "International Institute," I stole her camera and shot a whole roll of film of things like the moon, my feet on the back of a folding chair, a rock and other treasures. When I wanted to impress a girl, I always did something silly to make them laugh. When I returned the camera, though, Bonnie was not smiling. I spent the rest of the week apologizing to her with very little luck.

Bonnie always felt she was my "back-up girlfriend" when we were in high school. I would write her when I was not dating someone regularly (which happened one and a half times). Whenever my dating experience was over, I would begin to write Bonnie again. I still hear about that inconsistency from time to time.

I might never have known Bonnie as my wife was it not for a hailstorm that came through Red Rock and destroyed the wheat harvest for the Mullins family. Because there was less money to be used for college, Bonnie decided to go to nearby Bethany Nazarene College in Bethany, Oklahoma, instead of Mid-America Nazarene College in Olathe, Kansas. Meanwhile, my parents were determined to send me to BNC from the time I took my first cry.

It took a little time for me to get my courage up to ask Bonnie out, but she finally agreed to go miniature golfing with me. She beat me by one stroke, 53 to 54. Because we had such a great time together, I did not even mind being beaten by a girl. No, that is a lie; to this day, it bothers me to think of that missed putt on hole 17.

Once we started dating, we became inseparable. In January 1972, I bought Bonnie a "Promise Ring." I think it served as a "pre-engagement, engagement ring." It cost all of $17. Things progressed very quickly for us. It was not too far into our dating life that we began to talk about getting married. We even talked about getting married at the end of our freshman year, May 1972.

I was a true romantic when it came to proposing to Bonnie. We were sitting on the back steps at one of the BNC buildings. I looked into her eyes and said, romantically, "What do you think about getting married?" I did not have the ring yet, because I wanted her to decide on what she wanted—and I had no idea how a person chose a wedding ring. As we talked over the next few weeks, we settled on a date: November 24, 1972.

In the summer time, I usually worked with my dad on our farm. But as soon as I could, I would get in the car and head for Red Rock. When I was away from her during the week, I wrote her. I always signed off on each letter with "Your fiancé, Randy Schuneman." Bonnie later told me how she always laughed when she got my letters. Did I think she had another fiancé? I was in love, though. It didn't matter if I looked silly.

Telling our parents was the next big step. We would both be 19 at the time of the wedding. We needed their help. I broke it to my dad by asking, "What would you think about Bonnie and me getting married?" He nearly wrecked the pickup.

On November 24, 1972, we had a beautiful wedding in Bonnie's home church of Ponca City First Church of the Nazarene. After a near perfect wedding and reception, we drove off in my 1970 white Impala originally headed to the exotic honeymoon spot of—wait for it—Bartlesville, Oklahoma. Bartlesville is a lovely community, but it is not on the Top Ten list of great honeymoon spots. The wedding was held on a Friday. We had to be back in college on Tuesday. To make matters worse, it sleeted the night of the wedding. We ended up in—wait for it—Ponca City, Oklahoma. My dad made reservations at the same motel where some of Bonnie's relatives were staying!

We were able to make it to Bartlesville on Saturday. We went bowling, ate pizza and on Sunday attended Bartlesville First Church of the Nazarene for our first church service as a married couple. After the service was over, we made our way back to our apartment to begin our life together.

I could write volumes of books about Bonnie. God could not have selected a better partner for me. I was a man-child when Bonnie married me, like Tarzan except without the muscles, or courage—and I am afraid of heights and animals. Bonnie was like Jane. She loved me in spite of my flaws, trained me to be less immature and stood beside me even when she knew she would end up being a "pastor's wife." Actually, I think she was hoping that I would change my mind about being a pastor sometime before I graduated from Seminary.

I married Bonnie because she was beautiful, she played piano (a requirement in those days to be a pastor's wife), she laughed at my jokes, she liked me, she loved me and she said, "Yes!" As much as I loved her, I had no idea how blessed I would be to have Bonnie as my wife. She was

3

the best thing that God ever gave this country boy. She made me the man I am today. I am a better person because of it.

Through Jennie's trials, I saw a side of Bonnie that I did not know existed; she is tougher than a Marine when she needs to be. When Jennie needed to know someone "had her back," she never had to question that Mom was there.

I Should Have Known She Was an Angel

JENNIFER DAWN SCHUNEMAN was born on April 21, 1978 at Research Medical Center in Kansas City, Missouri. She weighed in at eight pounds and eleven ounces and was twenty inches long. Jennie's arrival came after Bonnie had experienced over twelve hours of very hard labor.

We had gone through all the birthing classes. We learned all the different breathing techniques that were to be used at each stage of delivery. I am pretty sure that we finished at the top of our class.

Unfortunately, anything that we had learned about technique went out the window when the first contraction hit. My "coaching" career lasted a record two minutes. I quickly realized that my wife was becoming quite annoyed by my cheerful, "No, Bonnie you forgot to take your cleansing breath. Let's try that again! Just remember how we did it in class. Listen to how I do it." Lucky for me, Bonnie couldn't move her arms at the time. If she had been able to, I think I would have been the one struggling to breathe. Bonnie settled for the "panting like a dog" approach in order to endure the pain. I chose the "quiet like a mouse" approach for my own well-being.

After the first seven hours of labor, a student nurse came into our room to show Bonnie how she was progressing. Using an "effacing chart" which measure progress on a 1 to 10 scale, the nurse proceeded to give her update. She said, "When you deliver the baby, you will be down here at 10. Right now, you are all the way back here at 3." I do not think any jury of women would have found her guilty if Bonnie had "taken out" the nurse immediately! I am pretty sure we could have hidden the body.

Experiencing it from my perspective, Bonnie's labor was difficult for me as well. I hated seeing my precious wife struggling for her life in order to give birth to our firstborn child. It was exhausting to have to keep rubbing her back or arm. I kept trying to speak words of comfort while intensely watching a rerun episode of *Leave It to Beaver* at the same time. I am not a multi-tasker! I became mentally drained from trying to focus on Bonnie's needs without losing track of the plot line when Eddie tried to belittle the Beaver up in Wally and Beaver's bedroom. Give me a break! I had only seen this episode five times.

During the stressful night and early morning, I courageously endured the uncomfortable chair I sat in, an intense pain in my neck from trying to keep one eye on Bonnie and the other on the TV, sleep deprivation from not sleeping more than five hours or six if you count the hour I slept in her hospital room, and hunger. I hadn't eaten since midnight. I am no hero! I just did whatever a manly man would do!

But Bonnie didn't even notice the dire condition I was facing. She seemed so focused on herself and her own pain. I had to rely on the nursing staff to come to my rescue. About seven o'clock that Friday morning, one of the nurses came in and compassionately told me, "Dad, you are going to need your strength. Why don't you go down to get some breakfast?"

I reluctantly left my wife at her hour of greatest need, found a buddy who worked at the hospital and enjoyed a two-hour breakfast! (Warning: Gentlemen, do not try this at home! Your insensitivity will be a topic of conversation every time a baby is born for the rest of your life!)

When I got back to the room around nine o'clock, I could tell Bonnie seemed at little upset at me. I had heard how women often turn on their husbands during the labor process. As if it were our fault, we men often get blamed for the pregnancy. Not wanting any issue to come between us, I quickly forgave my wife of her attitude problem! I am too big to be small. Why should her lack of compassion for me be a barrier to such a beautiful event? I just let it go!

After ten hours of hard labor, the Doctor finally came into the room to evaluate the progress. He determined that things were still going too slowly, so he made two decisions: "breaking the water" which brings the woman to the point of no return and beginning a Pitocin drip which increases the intensity and length of each contraction. The drug is nicknamed "Pit." This is because it makes a woman feel as if she has just been dropped into the pit of hell! There was no pain medicine used at that time. Along with her "dog panting," Bonnie also began some mild screaming! I gently tried to convince Bonnie her screaming might be offensive to the nurses. This also did not work well.

Then the time finally came! I was allowed in the delivery room to watch that miraculous moment when a baby is born. The equipment to determine gender long before the actual birth was not in existence at the time. Therefore, we did not know whether our baby was a boy or a girl. Bonnie had wanted to have a baby girl first so badly!

I will never forget the moment when the doctor said, "It is a girl!" Bonnie began to scream, "I got my baby girl! I got my baby girl!" We were crying and laughing as we heard Jennie's first cry. It was so surreal to watch as the doctor cut the cord and the nurses began to clean Jennie up. Sure enough, this baby had ten toes and ten fingers! Her toes and fingers were perfectly formed. She also had very strong lungs! She could cry with the best of them. She would even learn how to cry at just the moment Bonnie and I were about to fall asleep.

They wrapped Jennie up and whisked her off to get footprints for her birth certificate. Without us realizing it, the nurses also took Jennie for her very first picture! You know the ones, don't you? The picture where every baby looks like a little red mouse! These little creatures look anything but human. They are wrinkled and crusted over. Most often, they have their eyes closed. That first picture is the one every grandparent shows to their friends, thus forcing the friend to lie.

The conversation goes like this. The grandparent shows the picture and says, "Isn't she a doll? Or "Isn't he the most handsome little boy you have ever seen?" The friend looks at that mousy little figure and answers, "Yes, such a pretty baby! He (or she) looks just like her daddy (or mommy)." If you really wanted to stay right with God, you immediately dropped to your knees and ask for forgiveness for such a lie! You know I am right.

Then, I saw the picture of my baby girl! She was the most beautiful creature I had ever seen! She was red, but it was the most beautiful shade of red . . . not like other babies. She was wrinkled, but those were just beauty wrinkles . . . not like other babies. She had her eyes closed too, but it was just because we could not handle the beauty of her baby blues yet . . . not like other babies.

I bought every picture they made of that shot. What else could I do? I mean, they were going to burn anything we did not buy! Perish the thought that the first glimpse of the most beautiful baby in the world would run out before everyone had a copy! Carrying one in my wallet, I would confront people I did not even know by asking, "See this picture? Is that not the most beautiful baby girl you have ever seen?" Unlike other parents and grandparents, everyone honestly answered, "Yes, such a pretty baby! She looks just like her daddy."

7

In those days, new moms got to stay in the hospital for five days. You could have the baby in your room or put her in the nursery. There was even a steak dinner served to the parents the night before the baby was taken home. I got the privilege of taking each visitor down to the nursery and telling them all the details about Jennie's arrival. I never got tired of telling the story.

Our family came up on Saturday to see our new arrival. My dad had forewarned me not to expect him to be a doting Grandfather. He had watched other men begin to talk baby talk to those little creatures. He was not going to do that! He did not want me to be disappointed when he showed no expected emotions when he saw his first grandchild. But recently I found out that he remembers where he was when he got the news and how excited it made him.

That Saturday, we had a large group of family and friends at the hospital. I noticed that Dad had vanished from the room. I went out into the hall to look for him and spotted him down by the nursery with his face smashed against the glass. As I approached, I heard him saying, "Gaagaa, googoo! I am your grandpa! Hellooo,little baby. You so cute! Yes, you are!" Okay, maybe it was not quite that bad, but Mr. Schuneman, one of the most feared school principals in Medford High School history, was totally disarmed by Jennie's presence. Dad just melted.

Upon closer inspection, we did notice one slight "flaw" in Jennie's appearance. She had a birthmark on her left eye. Of course, I had to explain to friends, "That is just a birthmark on her eye. The doctor says it will go away." I thought that my child might have the dreaded "stork bite." The thought of a stork actually picking up my daughter by the eye sickened me. It just is not cool to have a "stork bite."

As concerned parents, we asked the doctor about this noticeable imperfection. His answered changed everything. He said, "No, that is not a stork bite. Stork bites are birthmarks on the back of the neck. When the birthmark is on the eye, we call it an "angel kiss." From that moment on, I bragged to my friends, "See that spot right there? That, my friend, is an angel kiss!" Stork Bite? Very, very, uncool! Angel Kiss? Really, really, really cool!

From the beginning, I should have known she was an angel! We had already selected a girl's name five years before. Our first girl would be named Jennifer Dawn. Jennifer (or Jennie) was in honor of Bonnie's Mom, Jennie Bernice Mullins. Dawn was in honor of my Dad, Donald Eugene Schuneman. (If we had a second daughter, she was going to be named Amy

Suzanne Schuneman until we realized that her initials would be A.S.S. We did not want her to be an A.S.S. all her life. This never became an issue.)

The night before we brought Jennie home, I had a sleepless night. I could not sleep for one simple reason: sometime, in the next one hundred years, this baby was going to vomit! What if I was the only one home at the time? Who could I call to clean up the mess? Would my Mom drive those five hours to Kansas City? Should I wait until Bonnie got home and act like it just happened? Could I just hose this little creature down outside? She would not be able to "tattle" for at least two years. I tossed and turned all night long.

God has a funny sense of humor, doesn't He? The very first thing we had to do when we got Jennie home was change her diaper. She started crying. The only thing I knew to do while Bonnie was making the change was to put a water bottle in Jennie's mouth. It worked! She immediately quit crying. However, I began to notice that her belly was beginning to swell up like a watermelon. I had just enough time to say, "Bonnie, why is her—" when a tsunami of water came out of her mouth! It landed on the wall three feet away. My worst nightmare had come true! I have another hundred years of this? I prayed the Lord would deliver me from this parental duty. If so, I would serve Him anywhere.

Before we left Kansas City, Jennie was dedicated by my Uncle Howard Borgeson. Jennie wore a beautiful little white gown with a matching bonnet. Bonnie and I stood before the Lord that day and made a covenant that we would raise her in the ways of the Lord. We gave back to God what He had given us. We had no idea what that commitment would mean.

Six weeks after Jennie was born, we moved to our first pastorate, Olivet Church of the Nazarene in Wichita, Kansas.

My Eyes Adored Her!

BECAUSE WE NEEDED to supplement my pastor's salary, Bonnie began to work at the headquarters of the Evangelical Methodist Church located just down the street from where we lived. Having someone "babysit" would have taken up any extra money Bonnie would have made. Fortunately, pastors only work on Sunday and Wednesday night. Therefore, I was the perfect choice to watch Jennie.

In all honesty, the Pastor's Study at the church was tiny, plus to turn on the heat or air conditioning required using the sanctuary units. The church budget was so tight that when it came time for salary review, a five-dollar per week raise was a huge controversy. When the church was raising $22,000 per year, they were stretching the limits to pay my $140 per week salary.

Bonnie and I decided that I could work at home and watch Jennie. I loved the idea! After I finished my 10-page sermon outline, I had plenty of time to just observe my little angel! Besides, it does not take much time to see 53 people every month when they come from 14 families! I could visit in people's homes during the late afternoon and still take care of my other responsibilities.

Like any other good father, I was amazed at every little thing that Jennie did! The means of recording memories during the late 1970's was by Super 8mm film or Kodak cameras. We borrowed my parents' Hewlett-Packard movie camera for this important time in Jennie's life. The film for the camera was expensive and only lasted for 30 minutes. Still, I saw this as a good tool to record "the miracle that is Jennie."

Jennie fascinated me. At six months, Jennie began to sit up! I know, you wish your child had been so smart. One afternoon, I sat Jennie on a blanket in the living room of the parsonage. She just sat there without much movement at all. Every so often, she would lean forward to pick up one toy near her. What a Kodak (or Hewlett-Packard) moment! I loaded up the movie camera with a new role of Super 8mm film and began a 30-minute adventure of making a record of Jennie sitting up, not moving! Of course, this would be a valuable piece of memorabilia when Jennie was famous.

I got the film developed, brought it home and invited Bonnie to watch it with me. At the end of my filming "debut," Bonnie said, "Randy, she was not doing anything but sitting up. Why did you film her for so long?"

Obviously, I knew the answer to that question. I answered, "Because she is so beautiful when she sits up!" Surely, everyone knew the answer to that question! It did not matter to me when Bonnie made the point that I had used a "movie" camera. I found out later that the word "movie" comes from the Greek word "moving." There was supposed to be some action to this film. Poetry is not always in motion. Sometimes, it sits still for thirty minutes!

The only problem I had during those days was when I had to actually do something at the church. Oh, bother! On one occasion, two men came to lay carpet in the fellowship area of the church. I slipped across the parking lot from the parsonage to the church and let them in. I told the men that I needed to keep an eye on my daughter so I could only stay a moment.

The carpet layer said, "Yeah, I remember when my kid was born. My wife had not been away from the baby for those first two weeks. My wife and her mother decided to take a short shopping trip. I was left in charge of the baby. While I was waiting for the women to return, some friends came over to the house and asked if I wanted to go play basketball. I got ready, put my sneakers on and got in my friend's car.

My wife and her Mom passed us as we headed for the gym. They were headed home! When I saw them, it hit me that the baby was home alone. That was NOT a good night for me!"

I immediately headed home!

I will always cherish those years when I was home with Jennie. Most fathers do not get that privilege. During those two weeks in the hospital, floods of memories came back to both of us about those sacred days together.

No matter what stage of life she was in, Jennie always had another set of blue eyes on her . . . mine!

Bubba

OUR SON AND Jennie's brother, Robb Joseph Schuneman, was born May 7, 1981 at Wesley Medical Center in Wichita, Kansas. Bonnie was scheduled to be induced that day, so we arrived at Wesley at about 7 a.m. May it be noted that I never left Bonnie's side this time. There were no sonograms in those days, but our doctor had told us that he knew it was a boy. We later found out that he told every couple one gender, then wrote the opposite gender in his appointment book. If he guessed right, he claimed mystical intuition. If he was wrong, he would show the couple the book where the right answer was written down.

Bonnie was induced that morning and began experiencing intense contractions once again. We had completed another Lamaze class with all of its breathing techniques, but Bonnie relied on her more effective dog panting technique. I did not attempt to tutor her this time. I just tried to cheer her on.

To add to the intimacy of our surroundings, we were placed in a room with a young couple who were complete strangers to us. As we prepared for the hours ahead of us, it was comforting to hear the other woman sharing a blood-curdling scream every time she experienced a contraction. It caused us to feel warm and fuzzy as we realized that would be us in a matter of hours. Still, if Bonnie could have escaped the hospital, I do believe she would have made a run for it! If I had not left when Jennie was born, I would have considered sneaking out as well.

A nurse entered the room with what was called an epidural. The other woman was asked to turn on her side while the nurse placed a long needle into the woman's back. The needle looked horrifying to me, but a few minutes after the magical drug was administered, the woman became completely calm. In fact, she and her husband began playing cards. Every so often, the woman would place her hand on her stomach and tell her husband, "There was another contraction. I feel a little tightness in my stomach . . . there, it's over!" Then they'd continue their game.

Bonnie watched the amazing transformation in her roommate's demeanor, waited for the nurse to return, then grabbed the nurse by the collar and yelled, "I WANT WHATEVER SHE JUST HAD! AND I WANT IT NOW!" Before she cut off the blood supply to the nurse's brain, Bonnie let me pry her hands off the poor soul. An epidural was ordered immediately. A large needle, a short moment of pain, then Bonnie entered into the amazing world of near painless labor.

The contractions picked up, but everything was so much calmer than with Jennie. I escorted Bonnie into the delivery room while the delivery team prepared for Robbie's arrival. Our ob/gyn had another quirk besides his 100% correct gender predictions. He also liked to make a dramatic entrance into the delivery room at just the time the baby was ready to be delivered, not a minute too soon and not a minute too late. Unfortunately, Robbie had decided to enter the world whether the doctor was there or not.

The doctor knocked the doors open with his back and turned, then said in a panic, "Hello, everybody—*stop*! Do not let that baby be born yet. I'm not ready!"

Robbie's head was already clearly visible, even to my untrained eye. The nurse responded, "You better get ready, because all that is keeping this baby from being born is my hand."

The doctor did make it back just in time to catch Robb. As Robbie was being delivered, Bonnie asked, "Is it a boy or a girl?" The doctor answered, "It's a boy! I can tell by the ears!" I never took Biology so I was surprised to find out that was how you could determine the gender.

Bonnie and I chose the name Robb Joseph in honor of two people: Joseph George Schuneman, my paternal grandfather and Dr. Rob Staples, my favorite theology teacher. Dr. Staples had instructed many of his students, "If you name your son after me, always use a double "b." Otherwise, people will think his name is Robert. There is nothing wrong with the name Robert. However, we wanted people to know that his official name was Robb. Unfortunately, people still thought his name was Robert and our ability to find souvenirs with Robb on them was almost non-existent!

As they grew up, Jennie and Robb proved to be opposites in many ways. Jennie was a perfectionist who could not stand anything to be out of place. Robb was totally laid-back. As long as he knew where things were on the floor, it didn't need to be picked up, did it? Jennie could not stand being late. Robbie once told me, "Dad, if I get to school three minutes early, what will I do with all that time?" Jennie was diligent in getting her homework done. Robbie usually had his homework crumpled in his backpack long after it was due. These differences earned Jennie the title Miss Perfect from her brother.

During all the stress of Jennie's first illness, Robb proved to be our comic relief. He knew how to break the tension by doing or saying something that made you laugh. When Robb was two, Bonnie and I could hear him calling out softly from the back of the house, "Mama!" His little voice got a little louder, "Mama!" Then he yelled, "MAMA!" We rushed to the guest room of the parsonage to find Robbie sitting in the guest bedroom toilet with his head drenched in water! Somehow, he fell into the toilet, sat up to safety, but could not pull himself out.

While he was two, Robb went with us to visit my parents. My Mom scolded Robbie about some small action. Robb immediately fell to his knees and began to pray. How sweet, I thought, he is repenting of what he has done. I knelt down beside him to hear Robb say softly, "Get her God!"

On the ride home from church one Sunday, Robbie told me, "Daddy, we need to watch out for Elizabeth!" What was he talking about? He went on to explain, "You know, the Aunt of Christ!" I realized he had misunderstood the lesson on the book of Revelation.

Robb and I shared a love for baseball when he was young. He loved George Brett. I could not stand George Brett. Believe it or not, there was a time when the Kansas City Royals were a perennial contender for the World Series. During those years, they seemed to always play my beloved Yankees. I hated the Royals for that. My son came along and fell in love with my archenemies! You know what I did? I bought him every George Brett item I could find.

He always appreciated what I gave him, but he did not need the gifts. God seems to have poured out an extra dose of compassion, love and kindness on Robb. He has held me accountable in my preaching. He has taught me to face the prejudices I have and to deal with them. As long as we stay away from the topic of politics, we are the best of friends.

Robb spent three years in South Korea teaching English as a Second Language (ESL). From the moment he stepped into a classroom, his students fell in love with him! He started teaching lessons at a private school named Princeton. Instead of just teaching the material, Robb was determined to learn the Korean language. He wanted his students to know that he cared enough to make that effort. When he came home to visit, he would always pack his suitcase full of candy to give the children.

When he began teaching adults, his students could not brag on him enough. The married women wished they had married someone like Robb, because he was so respectful and kind. The Korean men became his fast friends.

The thing that blew me away was how Robb could function so well in a foreign culture. He could land in Seoul, South Korea after the last train had run for the day and find someone or some way to get back to his apartment. I think if I knew all the situations he got himself out of, I might not sleep at night. However, I would learn to trust Robb's ability at the most important time of our lives.

The Mischief Makers Club

Punky, Corndog, Pup and Ki
We are oh so mischiefy
In our work and in our play
We make mischief every day.
The Mischief Maker Club Theme Song
Words and Music by Jennifer Schuneman

EIGHTEEN MONTHS AFTER Jennie was born, Bonnie's sister Jenarold had a set of twins. Cindy and Mindy Jones were so identical that we first called them "the Indys." To the untrained eye, they are still identical enough that Mindy was mistaken for Cindy in one of Mindy's college classes. I do not believe they ever used their "twinness" to take advantage of anyone or any circumstance, but they easily could have.

Eighteen months after the "twinkies" were born, Robb joined the family. The combination of four children all within a three-year span would seem to be dangerous on its own. However, if you add the ingredient of mischief, things become downright life threatening!

Out of this combination of three girls and one boy was born *The Mischief Makers Club*. They had their own theme song. Jennie also defined what being "mischiefy" meant when she wrote the masterpiece, "Mischief":

> *Mischief is like a bubble almost ready to pop Mischief is like a song, floating through the air Mischief makes people laugh*
> > *And it brings you to everyone*
> > *Mischief can make the oldest person young again*
> > *Mischief makes you smile*
> > *Mischief is a treasure that can never be paid for in full*

> *Mischief is like a babbling brook . . . Mischief is universal . . .*
> *I am Mischief . . . You are Mischief . . . Mischief is Mischief.*

In real life, being "mischiefy" did not look quite so poetic. Getting these lovely children together had a synergy that turned four perfect angels into a force to be reckoned with!

Usually, the battleground was the office of their grandfather, Baba. With the door closed and their mouth silencers on, the quartet found themselves in the wonderful world of Baba's desk. Plenty of paper, pencils, paper clips and other weaponry made this room a perfect place to establish Headquarters.

From this encampment, all of the original musicals and plays were written, practiced and prepared for their one-night only performance for the family in the living room. The conversations taking place in the living room would be halted as the Mischief Makers prepared to perform. There were last-minute instructions and a short "walk through," and then the performance would begin.

If you were not one of the proud parents in the family, you might have thought the songs and choreography were annoying. If you *were* a proud parent, you knew it was annoying! Only joking!

The collateral damage was always Baba's office! The place was always ransacked as if a tornado had hit it. During one of the assaults on his territory, Baba drew a picture of a face filled with anger. He sternly wrote, "Get Out Now!" under the image. He laid it on his desk expecting this command would be followed.

When he returned to his desk, the warning had been turned over and Colonel Robbie had drawn a person waving a flag. Above the image, Robb had written, "Maybe I don't want to get out!" It was signed "guess who." On the flag the phrase, "I don't want to" was written defiantly.

To make matters words, the Colonel added these instructions, "Go on in Cindy and Mindy and Jennie and Robbie." This was nothing less than mutiny! Although I think Baba finally won that battle, it is still one of his favorite stories to tell. The drawings were kept for the "Mischief Folder."

This "Top Secret" folder contains a journal of the activity of the band of marauders. It also contained tons of memories of when this gang was together. It is a major keepsake now. Jennie kept it in a special place in her filing cabinet.

Of course, an army has to have special names in order to speak in code to each other. Jennie's nickname was *Punky*. Cindy was *Pup*. Mindy's name was *Ki* (pronounced Key). Finally, Robbie's nickname was *Corndog*. I have no idea why. There were a variety of variations from these foundational names, but these are the main nicknames still used today.

I had the "privilege" of staying up with all four children one New Year's Eve. We were sent to the old green mobile home about a half-mile away from the house. There was no television, no radio and no phone. I thought the night would never end! For my comrades, nothing could have been more fun. Just being together was a blast for them. It was a painful, noisy night. I got sick from the lack of sleep.

And I would not trade that night for anything.

What came out of this combination was four children who grew up as three sisters and a brother. They were more than cousins. They were "Four for one, one for four." They were inseparable.

The Mischief Folder will always be a prized treasure. Someday, my hope is that the next generation of cousins—Annabelle, Cayden and all the other nieces and nephews—will be able to sit down and read the biography and autobiography of a small band of renegades whom I love with all my heart.

Reigning Cats And Dogs

A Purrfect Friend

From a small, white ball of fur to a large, gentle giant,
Jumpy was my dear friend. He would play with me, or cuddle
with me when I needed a friend. He was a wonderful cat.
And then, it happened. Jumpy had been missing for quite some time.
I wondered where he could possibly be. A phone call
from a neighbor soon answered all my questions.
I watched as my mother's face fell and knew that I didn't
have to ask if Jumpy was okay. He was gone forever.
It was a small, sad group that walked out to the backyard that day.
My dad led us, carrying the tiny form, wrapped up so
that my brother and I could not see. We reached the
place in the backyard, and Dad dug the hole.
We all said something nice about Jumpy, then my father prayed.
He then pulled out his trumpet and played "Taps" as we all sniffled.
My father shoveled the dirt on top of my friend as my mother, brother
and I walked back to the house. I knew I would always miss him.
He was a wonderful cat.

Love Me, Love My Pet

IT MIGHT SEEM strange to begin a book about the grieving process with a section on household pets, but it is impossible to know Jennie without understanding her love for animals. She shared her mother's passion for the "little people" of earth. As you will see in the next few pages, Jennie did not care so much what kind of animal it was. She loved them all.

There is a second reason for including these chapters, though. I think you may find that some parts of Jennie's story will make you cry. If you encounter this book like I hope you will, tears will be inevitable. When that time comes, just stop where you are reading and flip back to one of these chapters. Cleanse your emotional palate and then return to where you left off.

One thing I have learned is that God mixes our sorrow with joy. If not for some of the antics that our family pets have put us through, life would be much harder to handle. If you love pets like Jennie did, you will enjoy reading about Isaac Newt-on, Jumpy 3, our beloved Sassy and of course Charlie, our Tasmanian devil.

If you do not like pets, please give these creatures a chance anyway. You won't have to feed them, keep fresh water for them or clean up their messes. Just pretend they are like your grandchildren—love them for the moment and then give them back. What could it hurt?

You might surprise yourself by falling in love with at least one of them. The great thing about these pets is that you can shut them up in the book, put them on a shelf and never have to worry about them until you pick the book up again. Meanwhile, I will be chasing Charlie!

Here Kitty, Kitty!

THE THEORY THAT cats have nine lives could not be easily proven through our early history with these furry animals. When our kids were little, we went through cats and kittens like tokens at an arcade. We felt great pride when our first cat lived to be a year and a half. In a short period of time, we went through three Jumpys, two Callies, one Pudgy, one Tina, a Tony and Duke, the funniest kitten we ever had, but who lost his challenge to an oncoming tractor.

While Bonnie and I were on vacation to Hawaii one year, Jumpy 2 got run over by a car. The accident happened close to one of our member's homes. Being the thoughtful person that she was, Faye put the corpse in a plastic bag and saved it for us. We came home to a white cat in a black bag with a serious case of rigor mortis. The only thing we could do was bury the cat in the half-acre field behind the parsonage. I dug a shallow grave, got my trumpet and conducted a full-blown funeral.

By the time we realized that it was illegal to bury animals inside the Wichita city limits, we had a good-sized pet cemetery in place. All three Jumpys, plus a Callie or two joined Paul E., the parakeet, in eternal rest.

For fear of legal action, I will not tell you where the "graveyard" is, but someday a bulldozer is going to uncover what will look like a mass petocide.

We never bought a cat or kitten. We did accept numerous "giveaways." The problem with free kittens is that you fail to listen to Bob Barker's advice about neutering or spaying your animals. Of course, this led to a number of "surprise" litters. One litter, however, was not as much of a surprise as I first thought.

We had been given a black and white kitten by some friends at Bonnie's work. Jennie wanted to name the kitten Pepper while Robb liked the name Junior. In negotiations worthy of Henry Kissinger, we compromised on the name PJ. PJ was a female kitten that grew into a "young woman" cat. I had never seen a cat in heat until I watched PJ go through this strange ritual. There was never a question about PJ's readiness to be with a male companion. Recognizing this condition, we always kept her inside during that time.

About the time PJ experienced puberty; a long-haired male cat began wandering around our neighborhood. He might have been a pretty cat, but his hair was always matted with dirt. He definitely had to be homeless, because no good owner would have allowed him to look so bad. We always referred to this vagabond as Scrounge. Scrounge never caused us any problems, but he was often lurking around our house. We usually chased him off.

One day, Jennie had her best friend, Yvonne Keelor, over to the house for a visit. The girls noticed two things that day. They noticed Scrounge was hanging around in the front yard AND PJ happened to be in heat! Jennie and Yvonne got the great idea to toss PJ out in the front yard while Scrounge waited nearby. When they carried out their plan, the girls got a very graphic sex education lesson! Animal instinct took over. It would not be long until we realized that we had a new "son-in-law" on our hands! Our family came home from Vacation Bible School to find a litter of four kittens cuddled up in the middle of one of our bedrooms. Two of their litter, Pudgy and Herman, would become the newest members of our family. PJ and Herman were a part of our lives for eighteen years.

I realize that you will find this hard to believe, but after the litter was born, Scrounge came to our house every Father's Day and spent the whole day. He spent four consecutive Father's Day with his "kiddos." When he did not show up for his fifth Father's Day, we figured he might have an "extended family" or two he had to take care of. Pudgy looked like his Dad. He was black with a white underbelly and long hair.

Bonnie promised me that when PJ and Herman died, we would not have any more cats. That was final! Our plan was going very well, until Bonnie called from her parents' 900-acre ranch with desperation in her voice. The call went something like this:

Bonnie: Randy, we found Momma Kitty dead out in the field. She had been killed by a wild animal."

Randy: Honey, I am so sorry to hear that. I know you loved Momma Kitty, but things like this happen.

Bonnie: You don't understand! Momma Kitty was pregnant last time we saw her. Before she died, she delivered her last litter of kittens.

Randy: Well, honey, that is wonderful. Kittens are so cute!

Bonnie: You don't understand! Jennie and I found the litter of six kittens after searching all day. They were in the hay barn. We rescued them!

Randy: Bonnie, that is great! I am proud of both of you for being so diligent in your search.

Bonnie: You don't understand! These kittens lost their momma.

Some do not even have their eyes open yet. Momma Kitty fed them well before she died, but they will not survive without help.

Randy: It is a good thing that your parents are there. They will be able to take care of those cute little creatures.

Bonnie: You don't understand! Mom and Dad cannot take care of these kittens. They do not have the energy to feed them twice a day.

Randy: What do you want to do then?

Bonnie: We are going to bring all six kittens home with us. Jennie said she would take care of three and we can take care of three. Of course, we will have to get little doll bottles and special formula and special litter . . .

It was about this time that I began to understand

One of my favorite pictures of Jennie was taken on the day they rescued those kittens! Jennie's face is red, her hair is a mess, sweat is pouring off her head, but there are two kittens in her hands . . . and she is smiling like she just discovered a million dollars!

I hate to admit it, but one of my favorite experiences was raising those six little kittens. I loved opening the bedroom door and watching them tumble out single-file. I loved bottle feeding them until their tummies were ready to burst. I enjoyed watching them play as they got older. We gave away two kittens to friends. Jennie kept Chloe and Grayce until she realized her dog Charlie was making their life miserable. She gave them away to good homes. Socksie was given away right before we moved to Edmond.

We still have Peter for now. He is five now. I promise that sometime within the next ten years, we will not have any cats in our home. Or maybe not.

All Dogs Go To Heaven

I REMEMBER THE first day I met her. Jennie was standing at the door of my office bawling her eyes out. My daughter wanted a puppy. Not just any puppy, oh no! Jennie wanted one of the puppies from a Dalmatian/Labrador litter. Although I always hate to see my daughter cry, I stood my ground. There were several logical reasons for my decision.

First, we had just moved into a brand new parsonage with new carpet, wood floors and drywall (drywall is a Labrador's favorite snack). Puppies have to be house trained. I did not want to be responsible for all the stains on the carpet.

Second, this whole litter of puppies was going to be enormous. Beth Bidle, our children's associate, had already taken one of the puppies home. Her puppy, named Cow, (so named because her coloring looked like a jersey cow) would grow up to be over 80 pounds and did devour a wall of Beth's house.

Finally, I did not want to have a dog. Jennie was down to a whimper when a friend from the church stuck his head in the office and said, "Anybody want a puppy?" Someone had driven by his daughter's house and thrown this puppy out of the car before speeding away. I thought, "Why would anyone want a throw away puppy?"

Then I saw her, the cutest dog I had ever seen. She was a Cocker Spaniel mix. Her little bark only added to how adorable she was. She came with her first toy, a "cheerio." The toy was circle-shaped and could be thrown like a Frisbee. She would take off like a rocket when the toy was tossed. When she ran with every ounce of energy in her body, my heart melted. I had to fight off everyone else who happened to be in the building in order to claim that prize for my daughter and instantly, I was transformed into a dog lover. Before the day was over, we had our first family puppy, Sassafrass Schuneman—Sassy—a.k.a. Angel Puppy (sent from God above).

At the very beginning, Sassy was Jennie's dog. Jennie took good care of the new responsibility. Not only did she make sure the puppy had food and water, but Jennie began to teach Sassy some tricks. Soon, Sassy was rolling over, barking softly, barking loudly, shaking paws and laying down on command. Her most impressive trick was called "Bang!" When Sassy lay down after doing all her tricks, Jennie would give the command "Bang!" causing Sassy to fall over and play dead. Jennie enjoyed showing all her friends what her new puppy could do.

It did not take long for the whole family to quickly adopt this little fur ball. Because it was our first family puppy, we did have some adjustments to make. First, Sassy had to be kept in her cage when we were not at home and at night. She needed a little coaxing to get into the cage, but the problems really began *after* she was in the cage. She despised it. Even with a blanket over her cage, our Angel Puppy would begin a devilish bark and howl all night long. When we did let her out, she would immediately wet on the floor. It would take a year before we could trust Sass to stay outside the cage, and about six years before she began sleeping between Bonnie and me every night. Routinely, Sass would jump up on the bed, place herself on 60% of Bonnie's pillow, give a big sigh and fall asleep. Bonnie loved having Sassy's back up against her own. This left Sassy's paws available to be in my back. I got used to "repositioning" the puppy every night before I could go to sleep. As Sassy got older, we had to help her up on the bed. I must admit that it began an enjoyable part of my preparation for sleep when Sassy snuggled in. For her last ten years, we always had a "One Dog Night."

Second, we had to remember that after a dog eats and drinks, it will need to go outside. This is not a natural response for puppies. We apparently confused Sass somehow, because she thought she was supposed to stay *outside* the cage and relieve herself *inside* the house. Her favorite places were always on the new warm, dry, light tan carpet. You see, Sassy was a very smart dog. She understood how convenient it would be for us to scrub a little carpet rather than to go outside on a cold Michigan night. At the time, our family lived in a parsonage located on 30 acres of woods. I can honestly say that Sassy left the woods in pristine condition.

The most difficult trait that Sassy had was that the Cocker Spaniel in her made her a "runner." Up until this trait showed up, I loved taking Sassy outside with me when I went outside. She would stay right by. Even if she strayed a little bit, it was easy to spot her white-tipped tail waving above the tall grass.

Then, it happened! We were in the backyard with 30 acres of woods around us. Sassy got a new look in her eyes. She glanced at me for one last time, and then took off full blast in the opposite direction. The first time it happened, I was caught completely off-guard. I hopelessly watched as Sassy became a fast-moving speck down our road. She ran into the nearby subdivision and disappeared. What do you do when a puppy just takes off? You get in your car and keep driving until you see something moving. It was good that Sassy would get in the car when we caught up to her. Surely, this was a fluke! It was even sort of cute when you think about it.

Over the next sixteen years, her running became less and less funny. She had to wear a leash if she was going outside. If not, you were going to chase her. I found her inside the grade school building down the road. Children had gathered around so she was easy to catch. I found her wandering around in our neighbors' yards, especially if they had a dog. You could tell it was coming every time, but there was nothing that could be done to stop her once she set her mind on running.

When Jennie went off to college, Sassy became Bonnie's dog. They were inseparable. I often said, "Bonnie, if you ever have to choose between Sassy and me, I know I am a goner! If I believed in Reincarnation, I would choose to come back as Sassy, because no one has ever been loved more."

Sass began to develop arthritis and was unable to jump on the bed as easily. It was hard to watch her suffer, but we hated the thought of her being gone. Knowing that the day would soon come, Jennie made Bonnie promise to keep Charlie, Jennie's puppy, for her. Jennie said, "You know why I want you to keep Charlie, don't you? When Sassy dies, I'll be there to take care of her. And you will be here to take care of Charlie."

On Tuesday, February 1, 2011, Bonnie and I woke up to a beautiful sunny day. While Bonnie and I were having coffee, Bonnie said, "I think I can do it. I think I can put Sassy to sleep today. If I can handle the loss of my daughter and my mother, I can do this!"

As we drove to the vet's office for one last time, I asked Bonnie, "How are you able to handle this?"

Bonnie said, "Just don't think about it."

We both walked Sassy up to the office door. For some reason, I thought it would be as easy as giving Sassy to the veterinarian and walking away. I became quite uncomfortable as I realized the doctor was drawing the poison as we walked in to the room. I quickly excused myself, but Bonnie showed her unusual strength once again as she held Sassy's head in her hands as Sassy quietly passed away. Sassy was gone even before the shot was completed.

The ride home was quiet until Bonnie said, "I wish that Jennie had died so quietly. Sassy just quit breathing." I understood exactly what she meant.

Sassy completely changed my attitude towards pets. Jennie and Bonnie taught me to love those "little creatures" that God blesses us with. There was a time when I firmly did not believe that animals went to heaven. I am not sure this is theologically accurate, but all I could picture was Sassy waking up in Jennie's arms. For it to be heaven, Sassy would have to be a puppy again. I can picture Jennie and Sassy running through some field together in heaven. This time, Sassy would never run away!

Good-bye Angel Puppy!

Sorry, Charlie!

WE HAD NOT planned to have any more children. Between our four family members, we had two children, four cats, one dog and a rabbit. That seemed to be more than enough. It never crossed my mind our lives would be so greatly changed by our next "adoption."

Our new adoptee entered our family under tragic circumstances. Earlier in the day, our great-niece's dog had been hit by a car and killed. Kenzie would be home at midnight from a band trip. Something had to be done to find a "replacement" dog. There was a frantic search of the newspaper ads which led to contact with two owners of "traveling puppy mills." The search was on!

This decision became an extended family adventure. Bonnie, Jennie and I would be a part of the gang that met the first breeder in the parking lot of a convenience store. Buying a puppy and doing a drug deal both feel a little shady. I served as a self-appointed look out.

The first candidates were two solid black Shih Tzu Poodle mutts. The breed is known as a Shitzapoo (pronounced very carefully). But neither of these dogs were just right.

The perfect replacement was found at the next stop. A deal was struck and completed, so I thought our task was finished. I did not know that my daughter had fallen in love with the black Shitzapoos. Silently, Jennie began to do the math. She said, "Should I get one of those puppies or should I get both? It's only $75 more for both."

She continued, "I have the money, but do I have the time? And what about the cats?" Jennie was known for her calculated decisions. She did all of calculations out loud. You could hear the struggle going on in her mind and heart. As we were driving, Jennie did something unusual for her. She made a spontaneous decision. She cried out, "We must go back! I want one of those black puppies!"

We made a U-turn and headed for a motel parking lot in Chandler, Oklahoma. There, a deal was struck to sell one puppy for $125 or both for $200. Seeing my wife's eyes beginning to have that "the second puppy is only $75" look, I was thankful that we only came away with one pup.

I found myself sitting in the back seat of the car with a little ball of curly, black fur sleeping on my lap. My heart also began to melt as I observed how innocent and cute this eight-week old puppy appeared to be. Jennie was always the family "worrier." She began to worry that she might have chosen the wrong dog. Jennie asked, "What if all he does is lay around? What if he is not playful? What if he sleeps all the time?" Charlie soon proved that Jennie had no reason for concern.

Charles Mischief Schuneman was anything but lethargic. Charlie soon began to live up to his middle name. It seemed that he only slept so he could dream about new ways to get into trouble. He loved to chew things like iPods, earphones, shoes, socks, books and one pair of eye glasses. Anything left within reach was "fair game." We prayed that Charlie would fall asleep during the day, because we knew our earthly possessions would be safe for the moment.

The greatest concern came from Charlie's love for chasing. It did not matter if he was the "chaser" or the "chasee," as long as there was chasing involved. This characteristic made Charlie extremely dangerous if he "escaped" through the front door. All bets were off as to which direction he would go or how long it would take to catch him. One could plan on spending anywhere from forty-five minutes to up to three hours in "hot pursuit."

Jennie decided to address the bad habit of running away by purchasing a "behavioral modification collar." She researched thoroughly to find the best collar she could find. The model she finally selected had a "buzz" feature which only produced sound. Although we never referred to it as a "shock collar," the apparatus did have an "electrical pulse" feature.

Like Sassy, Jennie was able to teach Charlie seven tricks on her command. Charlie could roll over, speak, beg, play dead among other things, like "beg to bang" which was a combination of tricks that, like Sassy, ended with Charlie playing dead.

Jennie was the best caregiver you can imagine. Unfortunately, there were tough times, too. The first time, Jennie called us in full panic. She was crying so hard that it was difficult to understand her when she said, "Charlie got sprayed by a skunk. What do I do?" She could not leave him in his present condition, but she did not know how to deal with the odor if he came inside.

Being the loving dog owner that she was, she followed instructions by going to the local grocery store and buying two or three bottles of Massengil, some vinegar and other home remedies. As Jennie recounted the story, she found herself standing in the grocery line holding some "unmentionables" and smelling like skunk from head to toe. Now, that's love!

Along with the seven tricks Charlie knew, he could also talk. In fact, every canine in Bonnie's side of the family is a "talking dog." It started with his cousin, Princess. Her opening statement was, "Whooo is Dis?" Daisy, the love of Charlie's life, began her conversations with, "What the hay?" When Jennie was going to work late, Charlie called Bonnie to ask, "Uh, Grandmaw, can I come over to Grandmaw's Day Care? I am lonely!"

The routine is that the caller must speak to the dog for at least the first three minutes. Then, and only then, will the owner come on the line. Charlie "spoke" with a very heavy Southern accent. Whether he is a soprano or a bass depended on who Charlie was "channeling" through. He could speak any time he wants to, even when he was not present. You see, Charlie even had a "satellite phone" to defend himself if someone was talking bad about him.

Needless to say, Jennie loved Charlie with all of her heart. She loved him enough to give her two hand-raised, bottle-fed cats away to good homes. Charlie and Jennie became inseparable.

One of the biggest losses Jennie felt while in the hospital in Bartlesville was not seeing Charlie. Of course, the hospital had a standing policy about no pets in the facilities, but that did not curtail Jennie's desire to see her dog. She had been so sick. It had been so long! Surely something could be done. If we asked for our pup to come to fifth floor, we just knew the answer would be, "Sorry, Charlie!"

Enter our good friends Buddy and Dana Stefanoff. Buddy had been a member of the Big Red 1 special ops force during Operation Desert Storm. This man had been chased by three hundred Iraqi soldiers for three days during that war, and survived. His Desert Storm experiences would make your hair curl. He goes to the shooting range to fire his semi-automatic rifles as part of his birthday parties, Thanksgiving and Christmas. If I was ever threatened, I would want Buddy Stefanoff to be beside me—if not in front of me. The word "impossible" does not show up in Buddy's vocabulary very often. Getting Charlie into the hospital room? No problem!

Buddy and Dana concocted a plan that included secretive and stealthy moves. They put Charlie in a pet carrier and carried him up to Jennie's room! Okay, that may not be an episode of "Mission Impossible," but it worked. They did get confronted by a man while they were on the elevator going up to the room. The very intelligent man looked at Buddy and said, "That is a dog!" Buddy responded, "No, this is not a dog. It is a computer!"

The man hurried to find a nurse he could tell. The floor nurse, knowing it was a "guest" for Jennie, looked over and said, "Sir, you are mistaken. That is a computer if I have ever seen one." The "computer" was snuck in and out by the very same manner. We found other methods like blankets and coats to hide Charlie, but he made numerous visits to the hospital over those two weeks in Bartlesville.

Charlie was a special guest at Jennie's surprise birthday party. He was also with us on Jennie's real birthday. He is a living reminder of Jennie.

We could never let him go.

Bad Cell Connections

A Lifetime of Friendship

To a 4-year-old with terminal cancer, you were a good friend, Pooh.
Many days in the hospital were spent watching videos of you.
I survived, and ever since you've held a special place in my heart.
And even as I've grown older, we've never grown apart.
And another friend has joined our duo, she's a good friend of yours, too.
Our friendship is filled with lots of memories,
and even an adventure or two!
I thank you both for sticking with me through
times both thick and thin.
It just goes to show how your life can change when
you're blessed with wonderful friends.

You Are One in Three Million

ON SATURDAY, MAY 13, 1982, the weather in Wichita, Kansas was sunny with a light breeze blowing. It couldn't have been more beautiful outside. A friend from church and I had planned to play tennis at a nearby park. Bonnie was taking care of one-year-old Robb, so I took Jennie with me to the park. Although she was usually very easy to take care of, Jennie kept coming over to me to complain that her "tummy" hurt. Her interruptions became so frequent that I finally decided to take her home. I hate to admit it, but I was upset that Jennie had disturbed my schedule.

Since it was 1 p.m., I thought that Jennie was just hungry, but food did not sound good to her. Looking back, both Bonnie and I remember Jennie complaining about a little stomach pain sometimes after she ate. When we got home, Jennie's pain intensified. I had no idea that the pain she was experiencing was equal to a massive heart attack! I drew Jennie a bath, thinking that soaking in the warm water might make her hurt less. What do fathers know?

When Bonnie got home, her motherly instinct was convinced that Jennie's physical problem was more than the flu. We rushed Jennie over to the Emergency Room at a local hospital. After some tests and a lot of waiting, the doctor came back with a diagnosis: the flu! We took Jennie home and tried to keep her comfortable. That proved to be an impossible task. Jennie was still deathly sick on Sunday. While I went on to church, Bonnie stayed home with Jennie and Robbie. Of course, I requested prayer on Jennie's behalf, but I had no idea that my life was about to change forever!

Determined to see our pediatrician, Bonnie kept calling his phone service and demanding that the doctor see Jennie as soon as possible. Unfortunately, there was a major measles and flu outbreak that weekend. The doctors and hospitals were flooded with hundreds of calls from parents who described similar symptoms to Jennie's. Bonnie kept persistently calling until the doctor finally agreed to see us before office hours on Monday, May 15, 1982.

We loved our pediatrician, but he was exhausted by the tremendous patient load he faced over the weekend. It was easy to tell he was a little perturbed that Bonnie had kept calling. It was only the flu! He ordered some routine blood tests and waited for results. But when the doctor got Jennie's blood count back, his face turned white! He made plans to rush Jennie into emergency surgery at Wesley Medical Center, which was thankfully across the street from his office. A surgery team was quickly assembled. What unsettled me most was that all the medical staff was running; doctors and nurses running is seldom a good indication.

Within minutes, Jennie had been prepped for surgery and was being swished away by the surgical team. The *only* pediatric surgeon in the state of Kansas worked at Wesley Medical Center and was on site immediately. When we were told the name of the surgeon, I started to feel nauseous. The doctor had been on the local news frequently in the last few weeks because he was being sued by eight families for malpractice. Eight of his child patients had died after surgery. The doctor now had my little girl's life in his hands.

But Dr. Medo Mirza proved to be an amazing surgeon and friend in the days ahead. Over the years, doctors who saw Jennie's surgery scar would talk about how beautiful her stitches were. Dr. Mirza had been given faulty pathology reports and had acted on them. He was exonerated in every case. I did not know that at the time, however.

Although I was no expert in hospital procedures, it seemed like a pretty routine event. The doctor was 99% sure it was Jennie's appendix. We just had to wait for the appendix to be removed, the stitches to be sewn and meet our little girl back in the recovery room. Even if the appendix had ruptured, it would surely only mean a longer hospital visit. Everything would be fine. I was sure of it.

I intentionally kept quiet about the doctor's recent law suits. I did not want Bonnie to be more worried than she already was. It just so happened that a pastor friend from another Nazarene church was in the surgical waiting room. One of the nurses from his church came over to introduce herself and sit with us for just a minute.

The woman asked what was happening. Then she dropped a bomb. She asked Bonnie, "Who is your surgeon?" When Bonnie tried to pronounce the surgeon's name, the nurse gasped and said, "Oh no, he is facing seven or eight malpractice suits!" If I could have gotten away with it, I would have choked the woman to death.

During the hours of waiting for the surgery to be completed, someone came with a form for us to sign that gave authority to remove Jennie's right ovary. Bonnie and I faced the decision of signing our daughter's future hope for children away. We had just a few short minutes to make the biggest decision of our life. Time was precious, because they did not want to keep Jennie open any longer than necessary.

Take her ovary or risk her life—what kind of decision is that for a couple in their late twenties to have to make? I finally was the one to sign the paper. The person disappeared back into the operating room.

When surgery is over, the surgeon is supposed to come and give his report. The surgeon is supposed to come out and say, "Everything went fine!" No one likes to hear the question, "Would you mind stepping into the consultation room?" As Dr. Mirza approached us following the surgery, he had a concerned look on his face. He asked Bonnie and me to accompany him to a small private room where we could talk.

"It wasn't her appendix," the doctor began. "Your daughter has a cyst that has wrapped around her right ovary. The twisting of the ovary has caused pain equivalent to a massive heart attack. Unfortunately, the cyst has ruptured. It looks like the blood around the cyst is fairly fresh, but it will make treatment more difficult. This type of cyst, a teratoma, is very rare. Teratomas are multiple-celled cysts that can include teeth plus a variety of other conglomerates. In order to get a correct pathology report, we are sending the slides off to a lab in Washington, D.C. It will take two days to get results back. The odds of this cyst being malignant are one in three million, but I must warn you, if it is malignant, your daughter has about six weeks to live."

This could not be happening.

Time stood still for us from Monday's surgery to 5 p.m. on Wednesday. Our daughter's life hung in the balance. There was a world of difference between benign and malignancy. Time to wait. On Tuesday, I knew Jennie was getting stronger when the nurses tried to make her walk for the first time. They helped her get out of bed with all the IV line poles encircling her. When she got to her feet, Jennie began to shake off every nurse trying to help her. She just stood still and had a "fit." She did not need anyone helping her. She could do it herself! That's my girl—Jennie's strong will would definitely be an asset. Way to go!

Wednesday morning, May 17, 1982, will always be etched on my mind. Surprisingly, I slept fairly well in Jennie's room. Then, between 7 and

7:30 a.m., I had two dreams in succession. Both included Jennie and nurses and medicine. The clear message was that the tumor was malignant, there was treatment and Jennie would be fine. When I woke up that morning, I already knew what the day held. Along with the dreams, God gave me Genesis 22, the story of Abraham and Isaac on Mount Moriah. I knew what was going to happen as well as I knew my own name.

At exactly 5 p.m. Dr. Mirza came into Jennie's room. He had tears in his eyes. He sat down with us, took our hands and said, "I am sorry to have to tell you that the growth is malignant." I know that the normal response to that news is for the parents to fall apart. Instead, the word "malignant" lifted the burden I had carried all day long. The doctor was crying. Being Catholic, Dr. Mirza said, "I will burn a candle for your daughter." I was able to comfort the doctor and tell him I already knew. It was going to be okay. There would be a cure.

Bonnie and I met with all the family members that were present. We told them the diagnosis and the room was filled with tears. Not understanding the intensity of the situation, I quietly assured everyone that Jennie was going to be fine. God had spoken! It was going to be okay. I had no idea how we would cling to that promise for the next two years.

Before the day was out, we were introduced to Dr. David Rosen, the only pediatric oncologist in the state of Kansas. Dr. Rosen happened to work at the hospital where Jennie's surgery was performed. Bonnie had two dear friends that had undergone experimental cancer treatments. The protocol had actually *fed* the cancer. Both friends had suffered greatly as the cancer became more aggressive *because* of the treatment.

When Bonnie began to explain that Jennie was not to be used as a guinea pig, Dr. Rosen interrupted to emphasize that he was not expecting Jennie to die! Because of her age, the ovaries were not active yet. This would stop the cancer from spreading in the same way it would have in a mature woman. Sloane-Kettering Hospital in New York City had come up with a new protocol within the last two years that had increased the survival rate from 27% to 82%. The treatment would have to be aggressive because of the rupture and the type of cancer, but the doctor expected Jennie to live.

A plan was put into place that would allow Jennie to go home from the hospital to recuperate and regain her strength. Chemotherapy and radiation would begin over Memorial Day weekend. We took Jennie home for some days of rest and then prepared to begin a two-year journey through her treatment. Jennie was going to live! How bad could the treatment be?

38

Dr. Doom

ON MEMORIAL DAY 1982, Bonnie, Jennie my Dad and I loaded ourselves into the car and headed over to nearby St. Francis Hospital. Although the surgery had been done at Wesley Medical Center, the treatment would take place at St. Francis. None of us had any idea what was about to happen, but this would be a very tough day.

Because it was a holiday, we had been instructed to take Jennie directly to the Pediatric Intensive Care Unit of the hospital to begin her chemotherapy. We entered the room and realized that Jennie needed to have a Heparin lock put in her arm to be used to administer the chemo. I am sure it could have been a simple procedure. We placed Jennie on a hospital bed so the nurse could install the device. The idea of "installing a device" into the human body makes one bristle. Jennie saw the needle coming at her and began to scream bloody murder. For four years old, Jennie she had a set of lungs! She began to fight with every ounce of strength she had to get out of that bed. It took seven of us to hold her down! We were trying to comfort her while the nurse instructed, "Hold still."

Because of the holiday, the PICU was being used as a recovery room for all the pediatric surgery patients that day. I watched a few older children be wheeled in to let the anesthetic wear off. They were totally out of it. Who knows what those poor souls had been through? Then Jennie began to scream! Every child in that PICU sat up wide awake! All seven of us had our hands full just trying to keep this filly from bucking us off!

The nurse finally got the Heparin lock in place when another nurse came in with word from Dr. Rosen. Jennie was not to have chemotherapy today, but was to start radiation instead. Her small body could not handle beginning both treatments at the same time. We took Jennie from the PICU to the radiation department in the basement of St. Francis.

The confusion from the change in plans already had our heads spinning, but then we met Dr. Doom. Actually, his last name was DoorenBos, but no one could have burst our bubble any more than he did. His bedside manner reminds me of Saddam Hussein! He did not explain the procedure of marking Jennie's body for the radiation field. He did not tell us that the procedure itself would be painless. He began the conversation by telling us that Jennie would be *deformed* from the treatment. I still have not figured this one out, but he told us that all Jennie could ever hope to be was a *social worker.* There is nothing wrong with being a social worker, but Dr. Doom made it sound as if Jennie would have no other choice.

After dropping several of these bombs, Dr. DoorenBos left and his nurses came to begin the marking process. I borrowed the phone and called Dad to tell him what was happening. Now Bonnie and I are both disoriented. First, the confusion about treatment and now we are about to begin *deforming* our daughter. What in the world is happening?

Thank goodness for nurses! The head nurse sat down with us and explained, "I don't understand Dr. DoorenBos's attitude. We sat with him at lunch. He seemed excited about this new protocol. Knowing him, I think he just hates the idea of radiating children so small. I'm sorry."

The nurses explained they would be marking Jennie's body for the *field of radiation.* The iodine marking would help them to know where to place Jennie for each treatment. They only wanted to radiate the area that was impacted by the cancer. It took quite a while for the marking to be completed. Then they administered the radiation. It was painless and only took about ten minutes. Then we were free to leave.

We got back in the car to take Jennie home. She seemed just fine. What was Dr. Doom so upset about? The radiation was time-consuming to setup, but it really seemed quite easy. As we drove towards home, I even told Bonnie that maybe this was not going to be so bad. I had no more gotten those words out of my mouth than Jennie, crying, started to vomit.

When we got her home, Jennie continued to vomit violently for seven hours. Needless to say, it was a terrifying night. Jennie finally stopped vomiting and fell asleep, exhausted. Over the next few months, Jennie would lose 10 of her 42 pounds from the reaction to treatments. Two years of this? God, how will we survive?

The doctors did not have radiation and chemotherapy charts that went down to 42 pounds, so they had to guess at how much treatment

Jennie could tolerate. They would end up using the lifetime limits of RADS and each chemotherapy drug. That fact would come back to haunt us two and a half decades later, but no one knew what else to do in 1982. Case studies for most cancer include hundreds, if not thousands, of cases to gain their results. The only case study available for a malignant teratoma included 10 people. Of those ten, five had died almost immediately. The doctors worked the best protocol they could and hoped for the best.

Not Again

THE DAY AFTER Memorial Day, we had to go back to St. Francis for Jennie's second of thirty-plus treatments. No matter how sick Jennie had been the day before, she needed as many of these treatments as she could tolerate. Once again, the three of us got in the car and headed for St. Francis. However, this time, my stomach was in a knot. How could we put Jennie through another treatment when she had been so sick?

I wanted so badly to just turn the car around and forget the whole situation. As we approached the final turn to St. Francis, God began to remind me of the promises He had made to my sister when she had undergone surgery for a benign brain tumor. He had promised she would be married someday—and she was. He had seen her through the treatments and given her back her health. I will never forget sitting at the stop sign at St. Francis Street when God assured me that, just as He had been with Judy, He was going to be with us. My stomach immediately settled and I made the turn towards another round of chemotherapy.

When we were leaving to go home that day, we met Dr. Rosen in the parking lot. We shared our concerns and confusion. He comforted us as best he could and encouraged us to stay calm.

The nurses in the Radiation Department would become good friends before the treatments were over. We still have a picture of the three of them. It became routine to get up each morning, go for radiation and return home to watch Jennie be sick.

People used to stop us and ask of Jennie, "Is her hair naturally curly?" With great pride, we would tell them that it was. Now that thick, curly head of hair was ending up on the pillow every time Jennie managed to fall asleep.

She was also becoming pale and thin. It was a struggle to watch her suffer so greatly, but it was the only way to make her better. And now, with the radiation treatments underway, it was time to begin chemotherapy. We met Dr. Rosen at his office. He introduced us to his assistant, Vicky. When we sat down to be informed about what would be involved in the chemotherapy portion of the treatment, Dr. Rosen started by handing us an in-depth stack of papers that included information of all four drugs that would be used. It also included the side-effects of each drug. Once again, our heads began to spin.

The combined side-effects of the four drugs that were going to be used sounded like the disclaimers they read on television commercials for some new drug. The list was overwhelming— for each drug. All of them would cause further hair-loss. Most of them would make Jennie sick. Most importantly, we were to keep her out of school if there were any outbreaks of chicken pox. Her immune system would be so poor that a normal childhood disease could kill her. With the enormous list of possible problems we faced, we began the process.

And once again, we faced the problem that Jennie's weight was below any of the charts the doctors used to estimate how much chemotherapy to use. With such a rare disease and such a small child, they would just have to *work with* certain dosages and see what happened. If the dosage wasn't lethal, they would adjust the amount as they went along.

School Daze

BECAUSE BONNIE WAS working full-time at the Evangelical Methodist Church national headquarters in Wichita, I took responsibility of taking Jennie to her doctor's appointments. Jennie was just starting Kindergarten, but she had started reading well the summer before. This enabled us to not worry so much about the days she had to miss during her kindergarten or first-grade years. It became routine for me to pick her up at school, take her to her doctor's visit and then drop her off at the front door of the elementary school. I walked her to the front door at first, but after a while I started letting her go by herself while I watched from the car.

Because of where we lived in Wichita, Jennie attended school in the little bedroom community of Goddard, Kansas. It was a lovely little town with a nice-sized elementary school and junior high and senior high buildings that were close by. Goddard was one of those small Kansas towns where you would have felt comfortable leaving the keys in your car and your doors unlocked at your house.

Goddard equaled safety.

Nothing ever happened in Goddard, Kansas.

I was taking Jennie back to school one day following a doctor's visit. On the short drive to Goddard, I noticed that police cars were passing me right and left. There was a combination of Wichita police cars and Sedgwick County Sheriff cars. I remember thinking, "Man, there must be something *big* happening!" But, nothing ever happens in Goddard, Kansas, right?

I pulled up to the front of the elementary school and waited for Jennie to walk to the door by herself. For some reason, that day Jennie wanted me to walk her to the door. She had made that short journey numerous times before by herself. I thought I was too busy to take the time.

"Daddy, please walk me to the door," Jennie said. "Please?" I said, "Jennie you can do this by yourself. Daddy is busy." But she wouldn't give up. She kept pleading, "Daddy, please go with me. I am scared."

I finally realized that it would take less time to walk her to the door than to argue with her. Reluctantly, I got out of the car, took her by the hand and walked her to the front door of the school. I didn't even notice that all the lights were out inside until the principal of the elementary school appeared from his office. He was hunkered down and running to the front door as fast as he could.

The man opened the door and said urgently, "Get out of here! There is a gunman in the building!"

I grabbed Jennie's hand, ran for the car and sped back to Wichita as fast as I could. When I got home, I turned on the television just in time to hear that a 14-year-old boy had come to school fully-armed with automatic rifles and plenty of ammunition. The principal of the junior high had tried to stop the boy. The boy shot at the principal, hit him with a ricochet bullet and killed the man. Two other students had been wounded. The boy was still at large.

Later in the day, police found the gunman hiding in a field next to the school. He later was convicted of First degree murder. Because he was 14, he was tried as a juvenile and served 7 years for the crime.

There is an obvious storyline dealing with God's providence that day for Jennie and me. How could I ever have lived with myself if I had let Jennie experience the fear of wandering the halls of her school with a gunman nearby? I sat with one of the church families from Goddard as the news came in about the principal's death. His courage had saved the lives of his students.

What a tragic loss for his family!

I hugged Jennie tightly as I realized how close we had come to walking in on a tragedy. I never let her walk into school by herself again for those two years. I began to see every day as a gift to be protected.

When the details of the shooting began to become clear, the story took on further personal dimensions for me. When the gunman realized that he had shot the principal, he panicked. He needed to get away as quickly as he could. He needed a car! Other than the teachers, no one had a car, except a young teenager from our church, Garrett Dunn.

Garrett was in the hallway when the shooter began to frantically look for a car. He stuck the rifle into Garrett's stomach and said, "Give me your keys or I will kill you!" Garrett quickly tossed his keys to the young man and began to run for his life. He was shot at, but not hit.

Our youth group had about 10 to 12 teens in it. Out of that small group, one of our students had been nearly killed. That was bad enough! However, as details began to be revealed, we discovered that the young man's "target" that day was another young man from the group. As all junior high boys do, Bobby had made fun of the shooter at school. The young shooter's intention was to go into the school cafeteria, find Bobby and kill him. Because of the principal's courage, the shooter never made it that far.

This was a decade or more before Columbine or any of the other school shootings that have been on the news. Especially in a small town like Goddard, Kansas, this type of event was unthinkable in 1985.

Thank goodness for an angel that persistently called for help and prevented me from making an enormous mistake. Jennie's life had been spared again.

Hair Today . . . Gone Tomorrow

ONE OF THE most difficult side-effects for Bonnie and I to handle was the loss of Jennie's hair. Soon after starting treatment, it started coming out in clumps. There was hair on her pillow, on the floor, in the shower and in your hand if you touched her head. Most cancer patients do one of two things about their hair loss: Buy a wig or buy a do-rag. Some more courageous people feel comfortable just letting their bald head show.

With Jennie starting kindergarten in a couple of months, we decided to look for a wig for her. The only problem was that it was hard to duplicate Jennie's color and curls. We found a brown wig that was as close as we could find. It was curled and made to look as "naturally curly" as synthetic hair can get. Because it was summer time, Jennie hated to put the wig on. It was hot and uncomfortable. She would wear it to school and church for as long as she *had to*. The moment it was not required, Jennie would reach for the front of the wig and rip it off.

One Sunday, we made arrangements to eat lunch with Randy and Sherry Brummett, one of the new families that had started coming to our church in Wichita, Kansas. Robbie must have gone with the Brummetts and their son. Their daughters, Angela and Stephanie, were near Jennie's age and rode with us. Angela and Stephanie had both seen Jennie without her wig. I know this would get me arrested today, but Jennie's favorite place to ride was on the armrest in the front seat.

When Jennie was comfortably settled in, she ripped off her wig. I looked in the rear-view mirror and saw that Angela and Stephanie's eyes were the size of silver dollars. I am not sure they knew how to comprehend what had just happened. I wonder if they were thinking, "Could that happen to me?"

Jennie kept her brown wig on her top of the yellow lamp in her bedroom. If the lamp was always off, this would be no problem.

Unfortunately, we did not realize that synthetic hair melts! Bonnie went into shock when she saw the melted wig hanging from the lampshade! We could have buried the brown wig in our little "animal cemetery" located behind the parsonage fence. Brownie could have joined Jumpy, Jumpy 2, Jumpy3 and Paul E. Whatever method of disposal we chose, a new wig was now in order.

Unable to find anything close to the original wig, we settled on a blonde with hair as straight as an arrow. It did not look anything like Jennie's real hair, but it would have to do. We made sure that this one was kept in a safe place.

In spite of the fact that the new wig was lighter, Jennie still hated to wear it. We were at Dairy Queen one afternoon. Jennie had left her wig at home. As only a young child could do, a child rudely yelled out, "Daddy, look at that little boy! He's bald!" The boy was too young to be held accountable for his outburst, but I did briefly think about asking his father to step outside. I took a second look and realized that wouldn't be smart. I evaluated my chances of fighting the mother, but she outweighed me by at least 40 pounds.

On another occasion, I was headed to a zone meeting of local Nazarene pastors when I saw the flashing lights of a Wichita police car. Jennie was not wearing her wig. Her shiny, bald head was glistening in the bright sunshine. When she realized it was *the cops*, she began to wail, "Don't take my Daddy to jail! Please don't take my Daddy to jail!"

The few times I have been stopped by a patrolman, I have always been defenseless. I'm not a pretty woman and I never have enough cash for a bribe. Finally, I had a "trump card" to use with the police officers. I had only been going 39 in a 35-mile-per-hour speed zone. I had a baldheaded little girl in my front seat. She is screaming in terror at the thought of being left alone in the car as her dad was hauled away to the big house. But No! I got the ticket anyway! We skipped the meeting and went home.

It was a great day when we began to see little brown stubble beginning to grow back on Jennie's head. Her hair is very short in her second-grade picture, but it was beautiful to us!

Jennie's hair grew in a darker shade of brown. She turned from a blonde to a brunette. We thought she would never lose her hair again.

Oh, My God!

AT THE TIME of Jennie's first illness, my favorite verse in the Bible was I Corinthians10:13. It reads,

> *No temptation has seized you except what is common to man. And God is faithful; he will not let you be tempted beyond what you can bear. But when you are tempted, he will also provide a way out so that you can stand up under it.*

This was my favorite verse for one simple reason: it was Professor Richard Howard's favorite verse. I admired him so much that I adopted it. I wrote the reference on my hospital notes. I loved to preach from that text. It has some great word pictures in it. I did not realize how desperately I would need to believe it until towards the end of Jennie's treatment.

One of the major things we guarded Jennie from was chicken pox. We had diligently kept her out of kindergarten and first grade whenever there was even a whisper of a case at school. There was a chicken pox *outbreak* during Jennie's first-grade year, but it seemed to have subsided.

We were told from the very beginning of treatment that because of Jennie's suppressed immunity system, chicken pox could be deadly. If she had been exposed in any way, we were supposed to rush to the doctor's office for a shot of a drug called *ZIG*. It had to be done within 72 hours of the exposure. If—and only if—the drug was administered in time, would Jennie have anything to fight the disease.

We were in revival services towards the end of the school year. It looked like we had made it through the year without incident Bonnie was rubbing Jennie's back as Jennie laid her head on Bonnie's lap. Bonnie felt some bumps on Jennie's back. They were small, but unusual.

Bonnie became immediately concerned that it might be chicken pox. The big problem was that if a person had already broken out, it meant that the 72 hours had already expired.

We called Dr. Rosen's office. Vicky advised us not to bring Jennie to the office for fear of exposing the other cancer patients. It was too late to administer the *ZIG* drug. We would just have to wait it out. Hopefully, Jennie's blood counts were on the way up. She would be strong enough to fight off the disease.

Chicken pox goes through a cycle of breaking out, then beginning to heal. From what I know, it usually takes about three or four days for the cycle to complete itself. On the fourth day, Jennie was still breaking out. When I say breaking out, I mean BREAKING OUT! Bless her heart; she was completely bald at the time so her whole head was exposed to view. She had thousands of pox all over her head, her mouth, her back and the rest of her body. The pictures we took of her during that illness still make me nauseous.

Jennie just would not not stop breaking out. On the fourth or fifth day, Bonnie called Vicky at Dr. Rosen's office and asked for her advice. Vicky said, "If she is not better by morning, bring her to the hospital. We will put her in an isolation room."

I went to pray with Jennie before she went to sleep that night. Her fever was so high that I could actually feel the heat from her body from two feet away. I bowed my head and prayed, "Lord, you have promised to never allow anything into our life beyond what we are able to bear. We are so exhausted. I do not feel as if we can go anything further, but if we must . . . please be with us." When I finished that simple prayer, I touched Jennie's forehead and it was cool!

The fever broke and by morning it was evident that Jennie was finally beginning the healing process. Her pox all dried up, but still we were not able to take Jennie to Dr. Rosen's office for a few days just to be sure there was no danger to the other patients. Vicky told us to just wait.

When we finally had our appointment, we carried Jennie into Dr. Rosen's office. Vicky came over to us and began patting Jennie on the back. Vicky then proceeded to lift Jennie's shirt to see what her back looked like.

Vicky exclaimed, "Oh, my God!" "What is it?" we asked, startled.

Vicky said, "I have never seen a cancer patient so covered with chicken pox. When you called the other day, I told you to bring Jennie to the hospital in the morning. We were going to put her in the isolation room at the hospital . . . to die. We could not do anything to help her. We were just going to keep her comfortable until she passed."

Two weeks later, Bonnie and I were in the grocery store. We ran into a woman we knew whose child was a cancer survivor. She asked how things were going. We told her about Jennie having chicken pox.

"Chicken pox!" she said. "My daughter was in M.D. Anderson Hospital when there was a chicken pox outbreak. She was the only survivor out of the fifteen children on the floor. My daughter never caught the disease. I can't believe that your daughter did not die!"

I am so glad we did not run into this lady two and a half weeks earlier!

Every time I think of that experience, I have to think that Vicky was right. Oh, it was my God!

Night Moves

I HAVE NEVER seen a Mother and Daughter who were closer than Bonnie and Jennie. I would describe for Jennie realistic scenarios then ask her who she would choose. For example, "Jen, if Mom and I were in a jungle filled with poisonous snakes, hungry lions, charging elephants and ticks and you could only save one of us, which would it be?" Jennie always gave the same reply, "Dad, don't talk like that!"

You see? She would choose Bonnie!

Bonnie had wanted to have a baby girl first. When Jennie arrived, it was like a dream come true for both of us, but Bonnie was the one who loved buying the baby clothes and dresses and frilly socks. Shopping for clothes was not my thing. Bonnie also had the added intimacy of breast-feeding. I was thrilled when I realized that I would be able to get a good night's rest each night while poor Bonnie had to get up and down. I feigned a sound of sympathy as Bonnie would get out of bed. "I wish I could take your place, darling, but I can't."

Although we both loved Jennie with all of our hearts, a mother loves to comb her daughter's hair. A father sees hairstyling as a "pull it back into a ponytail of some sort" challenge. A mother loves to dress their little doll up in matching shoes and socks and dresses. A father grabs the first thing that has a top and a bottom to it, regardless of whether or not it matches. A mother buys her daughter dolls and tea sets. A father buys his daughter GI Joe figures and Wii cartridges for use later in her life.

As close as Bonnie and Jennie were from the start, Jennie's childhood cancer brought them even closer. I came to realize when Jennie was diagnosed with the second cancer that Bonnie and Jennie shared a world I never knew: nighttime at the hospital. Jennie went into the hospital numerous times in Wichita for treatment of strep throat. If that diagnosis proved right, it meant an automatic extended stay in the hospital for triple antibiotics. I would stay with Jennie during the day, while Bonnie would take the nighttime shift.

For me, the nighttime was the worst possible time to be on duty. Jennie's fever would often spike at night. Everything looked bleaker then. There were no visitors, just nurses who came in to wake you up to see how well you were sleeping and take your temperature and your blood pressure. Sometimes vampires came in saying, "I vant . . . to suck . . . I mean, to draw your blood." But for Bonnie and Jennie, these night moves were a part of a special bonding time that drew them closer together than ever before.

In the daytime, I had the advantage of showing videos. At night, there was just stillness when the lights went out. After praying with Jennie, Bonnie would say, "Have all good dreams and no bad dreams!" Then, I am pretty sure they talked the whole night through. It became their special routine for two years. I do not know what they talked about, but all topics were on the table. Care Bears or Strawberry Shortcake? Winnie the Pooh or Eeyore? My two girls could talk to each other about anything.

So it was a natural decision when Jennie went into the hospital at JPMC and later M.D. Anderson that Bonnie would take the *night shift*. That was sacred ground! The topics over those four weeks were not as light-hearted as they had been 26 years before. Sleep was not as easy either, but those dark hours at night were cherished times when two BBFL—best buds for life—savored every moment.

I suppose one of the hardest things Bonnie had to deal with after Jennie's death was trying to communicate how special their relationship had been. Jennie had lived next door for the last nine months. Bonnie had taught her how to make peanut brittle and decorate her house. As close as they had been before, my two girls had enjoyed the gift of being together almost every night after Jennie got off work. She was a visible part of every day. There was nothing that Bonnie and I could have loved more.

Jennie's most important concern was how Bonnie and I would handle her death. There were certainly tears about dying, but Jennie told every nurse she talked to, "I am worried about how Mom and Dad and Robbie are going to deal with my loss. I do not want them to hurt."

Nothing could stop the pain from coming. My college Resident Assistant once said, "If you love deeply, it will hurt deeply." Mark was a philosophy major. What he said has stuck with me all my life.

Bonnie received a *double blow* when Jennie died. Bonnie lost her Mom in November 2007. Gammy was one of Bonnie's BBFL as well. Being the baby of the family, Bonnie had three years at home with no other siblings. Other than an occasional sleepover at a girlfriend's, Bonnie spent most of her time with her Mom at the Mullins Ranch in the countryside. They worked the harvest; shopped, got the laundry done, shopped, got groceries and shopped together the majority of time Bonnie was not in school.

When we moved to Bartlesville, Oklahoma, we were only ninety minutes from Bonnie's mom and dad. For about seven years, Bonnie was able to go over and spend time regularly with her parents. She was able to take special care of her mom. As Gammy's health deteriorated, Bonnie was able to help her mom out around the house. Probably the best thing Bonnie did was simply being there.

To lose her Mom and now her daughter was an unbelievable loss for her. With her usual grace and courage, Bonnie continued to take care of both of her BBFL up to the time they died. She stills cries today, but when she needed to be strong, Bonnie certainly was.

I have come to believe that a father reveals to his children what the *Face of God* must look like, either good or bad. A mother reveals to her children what the *Heart of God* must feel like, also either good or bad. That is why most of us ran to our mothers when we were hurt. We wanted someone to feel our pain and say, "Poor baby!"

Bonnie Sue Schuneman has revealed to both her children and her husband that the Heart of God is filled with limitless compassion, strength, courage, patience and love. Bonnie has a gift that not all people receive . . . a heart with no regrets. There was nothing standing between Bonnie and Jennie when Jennie passed. I do not remember a time in their life when the two of them had a serious issue between them. The reality of their love for each other was always plain to see.

Because she loved so deeply, she hurts deeply! I pray God's healing balm will saturate Bonnie's life as she continues her journey.

I Am Just Guessing

BONNIE AND I quickly became literate in many medical terms we had never heard before. Jennie's tumor had been grade 3, stage 3. It was rated higher than it usually would have been if it had not ruptured. We learned about CBA tests, platelet counts, white and red blood cell counts and hemoglobin, to name just a few. Jennie's cancer had a marker in the blood so they could tell if the cancer was becoming active again. We also learned that chemotherapy takes each of these counts down in order to kill both good and bad cells. Then the good cells would rise again.

While the doctors were trying to adjust Jennie's dosages, she nearly died four times—from the chemo, not the cancer. Jennie was admitted to the hospital for the first rounds of chemotherapy, because the doctors needed to keep a close eye on her reactions. In June, her platelet counts got so low that she was actually *sweating blood* through her pores. She had a light pink fluid on her arms. Platelets are the part of the blood that causes the blood to clot. Jennie was literally sweating to death. Nothing could be done except wait for her platelet counts to start back up. Her counts finally started back up, and the crisis was averted momentarily.

On July 4, 1982, a lot of family had come to visit. When they left, Jennie's eyes began to gloss over. I remember Bonnie and me holding Jennie up so she could watch some fireworks out her hospital room window. We both realized her condition was deadly serious, but we were helpless to do anything about it, except hold her and cry.

Before the two years of treatment were over, the doctors had "maxed out" both the Adriamycin and the radiation levels for the rest of Jennie's life. Those tools could not be used again. Added to that fact was the reality that Adriamycin affects the heart severely. Jennie would always have to be careful with exercise. We got her excused from Physical Education classes due to her health.

Because I did not understand the intensity of emotions that I would feel if we lost Jennie, I prepared a *pastoral response* in case I needed to explain death to my four-year-old. This may sound strange, but if Jennie had to have childhood cancer, she was the perfect age for it. At four, she understood what we were telling her, but had no concept of cancer or the seriousness of her illness. She did not seem to be afraid, just tired of being sick.

I do not know why I would have thought of this approach, but I was going to tell Jennie to *Listen for the Bells of Heaven*. I had a theological speech that I was going to share with her to bring comfort to her little heart. Indicating how clueless I was of the situation, I tried to share my *bell* speech briefly with Bonnie. That proved to be a totally heartless thing to do.

By 1982, I had lost all my grandparents, but I did not understand the impact that those losses had on my own parents. I nervously presented a couple of poems at my Grandpa and Grandma Akin's services. My Grandma Schuneman was the first person I ever watched die. Her death was very peaceful and it seemed as if angels were there to carry her to heaven.

Two months before Jennie was diagnosed, a man died whom I had visited in the hospital in Wichita. Loren Hafner had been in the hospital for nearly a year. I visited him fairly often. Loren and his wife Sandy had only been married for a year when he was diagnosed with lymphoma years before. Now they were raising two beautiful little girls. For the last eleven years, they had battled this dreaded disease. When I went to visit Loren and Sandy, I always tried to make them smile or laugh. I would tell jokes. I even asked if Loren had gotten a haircut when in actuality his hair was just coming back in from his last chemo treatments.

I prided myself in being able to visit this couple more than their pastor had. Then one day while I was trying to be funny, Sandy looked up from leaning over Loren's bed crying and said, "I don't understand!" I didn't have a comeback for that! I still kick myself for how out of touch I was with a family that was hurting. They were so nice to me in my immaturity. I still remember going to Loren's funeral and watching two family members have to help Sandy from collapsing in sorrow as she left the sanctuary.

One of the first visitors we had when Jennie went into the hospital was Sandy Hafner. I apologized as best I could for my ignorance of her situation. In response, Sandy was wonderfully kind. Now, I still did not have a clue about the reality I was facing, this time with my own daughter.

Fortunately, I never presented my *Listen for the Bells* speech to Jennie. Over the next thirty years, I would preach hundreds of funerals and still

I did not really *get it*. I cannot believe I was so insensitive. I have tried to personalize each funeral, but being a comforter was not my strong suit.

I was able to hold onto the promise God had given me throughout the numerous hospital stays, struggles with strep throat, chicken pox and other complications that Jennie faced. I do wish I would have been in touch more with what my wife and daughter were enduring. I just could not lay down my preacher role. The next time we faced the horror of cancer, I would react as a father, rather than a pastor.

I had a promise from God the first time that everything would be all right. The second time, I was not so blessed!

Nurse Jennie

The Twelve Days on 3G

On my twelfth day on 3G my cancer patient needed
Twelve antibiotics (Kettia)
Eleven antiemetics (Blaire)
Ten warm blankets (Jen)
Nine forced feedings (Bobby) Eight bottles of lotion
(Amelia)
Seven biological response modifiers (Mindy)
Six antacids (Kettia)
Five wigs and scarves! (Jen)
Four blood transfusions (Bobby)
Three quiet rooms (Anisa)
Two organ transplants (Mindy)
One round of chemotherapy (Amelia)
To help with chemotherapy

All My Children

JENNIE WAS A Pediatric Oncology Nurse, which I believe must be one of the most difficult tasks in the whole world. In order to do their job properly, each woman and man called to this nursing specialty has to be willing to fall completely in love with each child, cheer them on when they are doing well, hold their hand when they are sick and grieve for them if they die. They stand by the parents with tears in their eyes, because they "feel" every loss. The loss of a "cancer kid" is always personal.

The nurses that worked with Jennie at OU Medical Center and St. Francis Hospital tried to attend every funeral of the children who died. They wept openly as if they were family members. In a special way, they truly were! I attended the funeral of a wonderful young girl whose name was Marilyn Williams. Marilyn had put up a good fight before succumbing to her cancer. The sanctuary was full! The nurses all sat together in a group. I sat next to Jennie and held her hand.

I am not certain, but I believe Jennie read a poem for Marilyn. Jennie always tried to use her poetic abilities to bring comfort to the families of her patients. One of Jennie's poems is engraved on her patient's grave marker along with a picture of Jennie and the child. I was always so proud when the parents would send a note or tell us at the funeral how much "Nurse Jennie" had meant to their family. Jennie was not only a good nurse, but a living example of hope. She could talk to the children from a first-hand experience of the procedures and the fear that came with chemotherapy and radiation.

In spite of the long hours, Jennie was always smiling and encouraging "her kids." At one point, St. Francis Hospital moved the parking spots where the nurses could park. Instead of being close to the building, the nurses were asked to walk from one of the farthest parking lots. After a twelve-hour shift, Jennie would make the long walk to her car and begin the journey home. Once she ate something, got home and relaxed, we would begin to hear her "stories" of what happened at work for that day.

She had a special place in her heart for each child. Her refrigerator was covered with pictures of her with bald-headed little girls and boys. Jennie would have her arm around them and be smiling at the camera as if everything was okay. She could tell you the background of each child: what type of cancer they had, where they lived, how many siblings they had and how they were doing. These children were her "extended family."

Jennie usually introduced us to her "other family" around the dinner table. We were introduced to Olivia, who always made Jennie's name into three-syllables. It was not "Miss Jennie," but instead was spoken with the most beautiful Southern accent and came out "Miss Jee-nnn-eee!" It was not unusual for any of us to stop and say, "How are you, Miss Jee-nnn-eee?" I want to meet Olivia sometime soon, but I feel as if I already know her.

Another of Jennie's favorite patients was Jonah White. Jonah is a courageous young child cancer survivor. In order to save his life, doctors had to amputate one of Jonah's legs. Jonah's response has been to take pride in prosthetic that he had to wear. Jennie's favorite thing to with Jonah was to act like a duck at a shooting gallery. With water gun in hand, Jonah would watch as Jennie walked back and forth by his hospital room door. Every time Jonah shot at Jennie, she would act as if he hit her and reverse her direction.

We also cried for those children who passed away. Jennie's response was very similar to that of losing her own child each time she lost one of her "buddies." Her poems would be "custom-fit" to the life of the child.

Jennie ministered not only to the kids, but also to their families. One of the patients was even hoping that his single father would "take a liking" to Jennie. She had several parents who stayed in touch with her. She remained "Nurse Jennie" to every family whose life she touched.

Although she went into two different types of nursing in her last two years, Jennie was always a pediatric oncology nurse at heart. She was proud of her Certified Pediatric Oncology Nurse (COPN) qualification. She was good at being the presence of Christ when families needed His love to become visible.

Jennie had plenty of opportunities to "tell her story" to as many families as possible. When Jennie was in the hospital in Wichita, the pediatric oncology floor had an overwhelming amount of reminders that children had died. Although I fully understand why this was true, it seemed that everything on that floor had the phrase, "In Memory of . . ." engraved on it. The television, the video recorder, the pictures on the wall, the Book of Memories kept at the front desk and other items reminded each patient that the reality of dying was real.

Jennie's presence as a vibrant young woman provided hope for her patients in just knowing "somebody made it!" We have a recording of her testimony that we will always cherish. As the door opened for her to share "His story" in her life, it also opened up numerous times when Jennie could pray for her patients and their family. As shy as she could be in other settings, Jennie was not reserved about sharing her faith. Her testimony worked its way into conversation naturally since people want to hear a message of hope in times of trial.

One of my proudest moments was the day Jennie went over to a Christian school in Ponca City, Oklahoma to give her testimony. She had a PowerPoint slide presentation she had developed. She took the children through some basic information about cancer and then she told them her story. She did such a great job, and she felt good about herself. She just looked extra beautiful that day. The picture we took of her that day is the one that has sat to my left throughout the writing of this book.

To Jennie, nursing was not just a job, it was her ministry. There is no way to count how many lives she touched during her life. I believe that impact has only begun.

76 Trombones Led the Big Parade

ONE OF JENNIE'S favorite musicals was the 2003 version of *The Music Man.* It was one of those movies that she had totally memorized. She made us laugh every time she talked us through the "Ya Got Trouble" monologue because she could do it without a single pause. She loved the story line, the songs, Kristin Chenoweth (a native Oklahoman) and Matthew Broderick. She "encouraged" us to watch it several times, although we could turn down the sound and just listen to Jennie.

In a great sense, Jennie could have been nicknamed "The Music Woman." She had a parade of her own. Every time one of her "kids" completed chemotherapy, there was a parade organized in the hallways of the hospital in honor of that child's milestone. Jennie knew how wonderful it felt to have that last "stick." She had a special "baton" all decorated for the special occasion. Sometimes, she may have put on her red clown nose, but always "the parade of completion" was as big an event as she could make it.

With Jennie in the lead, the other children would form a "conga line" to follow Jennie down one side of the hallway and then back the other. There was singing and laughing by the nurses and patients alike. No one was allowed to let this special day go by unnoticed. She had dozens of pictures of each "parade." She would often describe details of how the celebration had taken place.

Nurse Jennie understood the emotions of that day better than most nurses or doctors. I took her to her last doctor's appointment at Dr. Rosen's office. We were in the middle of a cycle, so I expected the doctor to tell us when we should come back. One more round or Cytoxan in a few weeks and maybe then we could celebrate. Instead, Dr. Rosen came in, sat down and said those words we had all longed to hear, "We are finished with chemo!"

I couldn't believe my ears! I picked Jennie up and began dancing out the front door. There were no cell phones in those days, so I had to find a pay phone (conversely, there are none of those these days) to call Bonnie and tell her the good news. I am not sure she understood everything I said the first time, because I could not slow down to talk clearly.

We started planning a Miracle in the Making service. We got a big sign, television coverage and a full-house in attendance! How could Jennie possibly forget how wonderful that felt? Jennie always has this huge smile on her face as she leads the "band" of celebrants.

I am sure there are dozens of families that have pictures of their child's "Big Parade." It was just an unforgettable moment. Jennie was good at celebrations! She was not afraid of being looked down upon because she was "childlike."

She arranged clown outfits, juggling performances (she worked very hard to become a good juggler), music, dancing and whatever else it took to put a smile on her kids' faces. She was prepared to color with a child who was bored or not feeling well. She might go home dead tired, but she never lost her energy to celebrate each life entrusted to her care. She gave it all that she had to make a miserable situation caused by a miserable disease a little more tolerable.

I wish I could report that all Jennie did was celebrate victory after victory, but she experienced a lot of losses along the way. Not every child who "came off chemo" lived a long and prosperous life. Sometimes, the music of celebration was replaced by organ music at a church. Many nights, Jennie just came home in tears.

There was a stretch of time when I tried to show Jennie and Bonnie what I thought were good movies. They hated *The Pursuit of Happyness*, not because of the acting, but because it was too sad. I got a chill when Will Smith pumps his fists in the air in celebration of his new job. All my girls saw were the numerous moments of heartache. After seeing the movie by myself, I took Bonnie and Jennie to the movies for my birthday. They both kept leaning over and saying, "Why did you bring us here? This movie is breaking my heart."

Bonnie's definition of a "good movie" has to include:

- A Happy Ending
- A Wedding
- Richard Gere

Bonnie's favorite movies are *Runaway Bride* and *Shall We Dance?* The wedding scene at the end of *Runaway Bride* is the "kicker" for that movie. Richard Gere coming up the escalator to ask his wife to dance, is the clincher in *Shall We Dance?*

When I saw *Bucket List,* I was sure I had finally found a "winner." I brought it home for us to watch on a movie night. There is a scene in that movie where Jack Nicholson's character overeats before he has his chemo. Morgan Freeman's character tries to warn him, but Nicholson refuses to listen. The next scene is Nicholson leaning over the "porcelain throne" vomiting his guts out. I looked over at Jennie expecting her to be laughing. Instead, she is curled up in the fetal position weeping uncontrollably. I turned the movie off immediately and asked, "What's wrong, Jennie?"

She answered, "That reminds me of my kids when they get sick. I can't stand it, Daddy—please don't turn that on again." I never saw that movie through Jennie's eyes until that moment. It is a great movie, but one that I'll never show to my family.

For those parents who have lost children, please know that right after they see Jesus and greet family members, the crowd is going to step aside so Jennie can march up with her baton in hand and say, "Come on, it is time for your parade!"

Stoop-ing to New Heights

JENNIE STARTED HER nursing career at OU Medical Center on the pediatric oncology floor.

She loved working there for several reasons. First, as I've already noted, she loved working with her "cancer kids." She fell in love with each of them and knew every detail of their story. She colored with them, made them laugh, paraded with them and made sure she kept each patient comfortable. There are only two hospitals in Oklahoma that have designated Pediatric Oncology floors: OU Medical Center and St. Francis Hospital in Tulsa, Oklahoma.

Second, she loved working at OU Medical Center because she could get so many items with the "OU" logo on them. She would proudly display the OU logo on her bags, her jackets, her badge and everything else she could get her hands on. Until the last few years of her life, she was not a great football fan. She loved OU because I love OU! It was as simple as that.

But that brings us to the third thing she loved about her nursing career at OUMC—she came to *love* OU football! Her favorite player was Jimmy Stevens, the field goal kicker. Because he is a little short, we nicknamed him "Little" Jimmy Stevens. Every time #17 walked out onto the field for a field goal attempt or extra point, Jennie would squeal, "It's Little Jimmy Stevens! Go, Jimmy!"

Recently, OU played Florida State in a vitally important game. If OU lost, their hopes for yet another National Championship would be stymied. At the end of the game, Little Jimmy was called in to kick a field goal that would "put the game away." I did not actually see the kick. I just saw the reactions of Jimmy and Coach Bob Stoops. Jimmy looked like he had missed it. He hit his helmet in the same manner as a kicker does when he "shanks" one. Coach Stoops had the most painful look on his face until the ball went over the crossbars. Then, instead of rejoicing, he just put his head in his hands. You see, Jimmy HAS missed a few!

Fourth and finally, Jennie came to know and admire Bob Stoops, not as a coach only, but as a man. Many may not know this, but Bob Stoops is a "regular visitor" to what was Jennie's floor. He comes to visit the children who are fighting cancer and often brings some of his players with Michael Honeycutt. Jennie brought me a signed poster on one occasion. Coach Stoops also takes as many of the patients as are able to one OU football game in Norman each year.

One of the funniest moments I had with Jennie was early on in her time at OUMC. She said she had a gift for me. She pulled out a "Bob Stoops" autographed football (which I proudly display in my man cave). She asked, "Daddy, would you like this?" My mouth dropped to the floor. I squealed in a very manly voice, "Yes, of course I want this, baby girl! Where in the wide world did you get it?"

Jennie innocently replied, "I won it in the raffle for Nurse's Day at the hospital. Everyone kept trying to talk me out of it, but I told them that this was for my Dad. Here you go!"

After four cartwheels and two backflips, I took the prized possession (which came with a display case) and trembled at the thought of having such a treasure. I proudly displayed the ball along with my OU Heisman Trophy ball that was personalized by Steve Owens. (I am missing Sam Bradford's autograph, because he was not yet a professional—*hint, hint* Sam) and my Josh Hybels ball (even though the autograph has faded—*hint, hint Josh*).

Every time Coach Stoops came up for his visits, Jennie would come home bragging about how wonderful a man he is. Second only to the kids she loved, getting to know Coach Stoops was a highlight of her OU career. When she moved on to work at St. Francis, she kept all of her OU items. I offer my thanks to Coach Stoops for making such a great impact on my daughter and the patients she loved.

When OU played Missouri this 2011 season for their first conference game, Jones, Whaley and Broyles all played to their usual level of excellence. The one thing that was missing for my family was . . . Little Jimmy Stevens. I do not know if it was because of the cliff hanging kick that he'd almost missed the week before or not, but a new place kicker was introduced to the OU fans. The young man did a great job. I will cheer for Michael Honeycutt him in every game throughout this season. However, I need to be honest—I am praying for a closing moment when OU's bowl game is on the line. Down by 9, Landry Jones throws a touchdown pass to Ryan Broyles, who makes another acrobatic grab that is humanly impossible. Dominique Whaley runs the ball in for a 2-point conversion untouched.

With less than ten seconds on the clock, in my mind's eye, the mighty OU defense causes a fumble or intercepts a pass. With two seconds left, there is only one possibility for a win—a 75-yard field goal! Coach Stoops looks to his new FG kicker, but for just those brief moments, the future hero of the Sooners gets a small "Charley Horse." It's nothing serious, but it disables him from this one final kick attempt. Who do we turn to in times like these? *Little Jimmy Stevens*, of course!

Out on the field, Jimmy steps back and then to the side. The ball is snapped! Jimmy puts everything he has into it, but the ball barely makes it over the outreached hand of the defensive tackle. It appears to be doomed to failure, but then out of nowhere the Wind picks the ball up into the air. Magically, it begins to rise up . . . up . . . until it clears the crossbeam by 10 feet! Jimmy Stevens finishes his last game at OU by being carried off the field on the shoulders of his teammates. The crowd is yelling, "JIMMY! JIMMY!"

Jimmy, when this happens, just know it was more than just you. Jennie will be shouting, "Jimmy, do your best, and I'll do the rest!" With her angelic hands, she will gently catch the ball and move it into the air and over the crossbeams! Just look up and say, "Thanks, Jennie!" Coach Stoops, you can hold your head in your hands and thank Jesus, but do not forget to add the phrase, "and Jennie."

Oh, for those of you who are thinking that I am deifying my daughter, don't worry. There is a reason that God allows His angels to take care of tasks like this: He is an OU fan, but He is also a God who does not show favoritism. If His angels do it, perhaps no one will notice!

Boomer! Sooner!

Don't PICC on Me

WHEN JENNIE DECIDED to leave pediatric oncology, she began to research what nursing opportunities might be available in Bartlesville. She would be closer to family and much closer to work. There was an opening in the PICC unit. The acronym stands for Peripherally Inserted Central Catheter.

That sounds fairly harmless, right? In reality, this is a two-hour procedure used when there is no other way to get antibiotics or medicine into a patient's blood circulations. Although it is not always true, picc lines are most often used when a patient has reached the final stage of life. Many of Jennie's patients were in their late eighties or early nineties. Although she had an office in the Dialysis area across the street from the hospital, Jennie's work took her all over the JPMC hospital.

One thing that I loved about her job was the funky, blue cap that she had to wear. Because of the volume of her hair, Jen had to stuff her hair inside the cap. This made her look like she was a bicyclist racing in the Tour de France! When she took it off, her hair would be molded into an unusual pattern that I always teased her about.

Because it is an "art" to insert the line properly, it took Jennie a little while to feel comfortable with her assignment. Her colleagues, Treva and Susan, were very patient to encourage her and patiently wait for Jennie to master the procedure. The nurse had to watch a sonogram while weaving the line through the proper veins into the heart. After the line was inserted, a radiologist had to read the sonogram to make sure everything was properly done.

Although Jennie took a class to qualify her to read the sonogram, she had to wait until she had confirmation of her success before she could leave. This was not bad in the daytime when radiologists were on duty, but when the local radiologists went home for the day, the results had to be sent to Australia for confirmation.

Maybe I am the exception to the rule, but I do not know many elderly people who would enjoy having a small, flexible tube run through their vein. Do you? The procedure is not totally painless, the tube is frightening, the process takes 45 minutes minimum—and the patient was in bad condition to start with. Add all these factors together and you will understand why Jennie came home each night with stories of being pinched and cursed and wrestled and *inappropriately touched* almost every day. A few nights, I thought I was going to have to go up to the hospital and confront some 98-year-old men about keeping their hands to themselves. Jennie always stopped me!

With her warped sense of humor, Jennie would check the obituaries every day and say, "I did a PICC line on him . . . yes, on her . . . and that guy right there. I did not think he looked good!" By the time Jennie had some experience under her belt, she became an expert at doing PICC lines with as little pain as possible. Some people even bragged to me about how good she was at it.

Because of all the sticks she had received as a child, Jennie made sure her patients would hardly notice when the needle was inserted. Since I am a diabetic, I have to have blood drawn every three months. I was complaining how the last time I had gone to the lab the nurse stuck both arms and then did "The Search" for my veins. This maneuver includes inserting the needle, then probing the inside of your skin with the needle until you find what you are looking for. The needle usually hurts going in, but it ALWAYS hurts being used as a Geiger Counter!

Jennie asked me, "Dad, why don't you come into the lab at Jane Phillips? They can call me so I draw your blood myself." We agreed!

The day came for the blood draw. I went to a lab at the hospital, had them call Jennie and waited a short time for her to come. She introduced me to her nursing friends and prepared to draw my blood. I was looking forward to having my loving daughter helping me through a sometimes painful experience. She started tapping for a good vein. She prepared the needle. She inserted the needle and—*owww*! My hopes were shattered of having no pain. Then Jennie did the unthinkable . . . she started doing The Search on me.

Jennie kept apologizing, "Dad, I am so sorry. It just makes me nervous doing this to you!" When she was finished, she hugged me, apologized profusely and then fireman carried me out to the car. Okay, the last thing is not true, but I was looking for some sympathy.

The main problem with being in the PICC unit was the long hours. When a line is needed, it really does not matter whether you are supposed to be getting off or not. Some days, Jennie would not have any PICC lines during the day, but as she began to walk out the door, she would be called back for an emergency. Again, the total procedure took about two hours. If you were walking out at 6 p.m., this would mean you would not get home until 8 p.m. at the latest. She was always tired when she got home.

What being in the PICC Unit did for Jennie was allow her to go throughout the hospital and meet more of the hospital staff. She began to like not being on one floor. Not everyone knew her name, but most everyone knew "the girl in the blue bonnet."

Bottoms Up!

JENNIE'S LAST ASSIGNMENT as a nurse was in Endoscopy. If you are not familiar with that term, you aren't 50 yet. The meaning is fairly easy to remember, if you remember *"end-oh!-scope-ee!!!,"* you will never forget the definition. If you have ever experienced one, you will never forget it. I promise!

Since our move to Edmond, I am now going to a new doctor who specializes in Pediatrics and Internal Medicine. Therefore, I go to the same doctor my 3-year-old great niece Annabelle sees. Most of the time in the waiting room is spent with young mothers and their little children. Do you get the picture? An old man sitting in a waiting room with children a tenth of his age!

On my first visit, the doctor's first question was, "Have you had a colonoscopy?" I said, "No." He responded, "Would you like to have a colonoscopy?" That is like your dentist asking if he could do root canals on all your teeth! Wisely I said, "I don't know you that well yet."

Jennie loved being a part of the endoscopic team. She loved Dr. K and Dr. V. She loved the nurses she worked with. She enjoyed the rotation process where you had variety in your day. Although Jennie had to adjust to the quicker speed of this department, Jennie began to enjoy going to work without being tired. No one, I mean, *no one*, wants to have an emergency colonoscopy! That meant almost all weekends free, eight hour shifts and going home on time. She felt immediately accepted by the staff and enjoyed learning a "new trade."

Our family had to get used to a different conversational topic at supper. Instead of hearing, "Today, we had this child that . . ." or "Today, this old woman bit me . . ." we heard, "Guess who's bottom I saw today?" It is one thing to have a deceased person's obituary read out loud. It is a totally different experience to have the posterior of someone, maybe even someone you know, described in detail. That takes "probing into someone's life" to a much deeper level.

Most of all, she loved her boss, Kimberly (Smith) Betts. In the few months they had together, Kim and Jennie became great friends. Kim laughed at Jennie's strange sense of humor. Kim helped bolster Jennie's confidence and made Jen's shifts enjoyable. The whole department was more like a family than a staff.

I have thanked Kim numerous times for enabling Jennie to enjoy the final days of her nursing career. I have never seen her happier. Her schedule was manageable. She could go to church without fear of being called in. She felt loved by the whole department. No one died on her shift. It was great.

Kim and the whole Endoscopy department were more than co-workers, they would be a part of the support team Jennie would need for her final battle. Jennie always knew "someone has my back!"

If Jennie were writing this, I know how she would end this chapter. She would pour a glass of Coke Zero for everyone; hoist her glass in the air and say, *"Bottoms Up!"*

Room 591

My Heart Cries

Be still, and know that I am God. -Psalm 46:10

Father God, I come to You,
You know just what I'm going through, And since I
don't know what else to do, My heart cries

I can't pretend to understand,
This isn't how I had things planned,
But I'll trust the goodness of Your hand, My heart cries.

This world, it makes no sense to me, This isn't how it was supposed
to be, But I know You see things I don't see, My heart cries.

The night is long, black and dark, Lord, bring Your light
into my heart. Remind me that You're never far,
My heart cries.

Take my hand, for I am lost, Upon the seas of life I'm tossed.
Shelter me in the pow'r of Your cross, My heart cries.
Life hasn't gone as I'd hoped it would, I'm crawling now, where once
I stood, But God, I STILL believe You're good! My heart cries.

Somehow, in this valley floor, Help me find the
strength to soar Close to You forevermore,
My heart cries.

75

So here I am, upon my knees,
Please still the storms that rage in me
With Your gentle words of peace, My heart cries,
And my heart finds
You.

8 Day Week

A FEW WEEKS before Easter 2010, Jennie began complaining about pain on her right side. It hurt near her shoulder blades and her right lung. She had experienced pleurisy before and said the pain felt very similar. Oblivious to what was going on, we all shook it off as nothing serious. But Jennie's co-workers noticed that Jennie was pale before we did. They suggested she go see her doctor. Jennie finally did so a few days before Easter. She sent an email to her family and friends that read:

> *Hello, everyone! (Friday, April 2, 2010)*
>
> *I really need your prayers. I've been having this pain in what I thought was my lower lung area for over a week now. It finally got to be so painful whenever I breathed that I went to my doctor on Friday. She said my lungs were clear. However, when she had me lay down and started feeling on my abdomen, she said she felt a fullness under my right lung. She did stat labs and a chest CT— the labs showed anemia and elevated liver enzymes, and the CT showed that my liver was enlarged . . . could be from a variety of causes—an infectious process, hepatitis, some inflammatory process, or (worst case) a tumor. Right now we don't know what the cause is . . . just that I'm in a great deal of pain. I'm scheduled to have an abdominal CT and a liver biopsy done on Monday morning. The results should be available by Wednesday or Thursday . . . I know that God is in complete control, but it's still a bit scary (especially when both my primary and GI docs wanted to know all about what kind of cancer I had when I was little and what treatments I had)!*

We attended Easter Sunday service. Of course, I requested prayer on Jennie's behalf. If I had known what the next week held, I would have prayed for time to stand still. Bonnie, Jennie and I went to Jane Phillips Medical Center in Bartlesville for her CT scan and liver biopsy on Monday. When the radiologist came back to talk to us he said, "Part of the liver looks like it is dead. I am not positive what I am seeing, but there is definitely something abnormal. We got a good sample for the pathologists. We should have the official results back on Wednesday."

Jennie was in quite a bit of pain after the biopsy. We took her home and gave her pain medication. The meds would ease the pain some. However, when they wore off, Jennie was getting more and more uncomfortable. She has a high tolerance for pain, so when she complained, you knew there was a problem.

Waiting can be the worst part. The mind begins to imagine the worst possible scenario. That first week of April 2010 was the longest week of our lives. No news on Tuesday, but surely we would know something on Wednesday.

Wednesday came, no news.

Our Worship Associate, Darren Melton's last Sunday with us had been Easter Sunday. He was moving to Independence, Kansas to begin his first pastorate. I had asked the choir and anyone who was interested in being a part of the music ministry to join me on Wednesday night. I taught a short lesson on *singing from the heart*. I had the choir sing along to a Brooklyn Tabernacle recording. I gave them the words and kept asking them to sing it as they felt it. At the end of our rehearsal, I shared with the choir what I was feeling as we waited on results that could change our lives again.

Bonnie wrote an email update that read:

> *Jen is off work the rest of the week. She has no energy and the pain seems to never stop. Her boss, Kim (Smith) Betts, is going "above and beyond." It helps that Jen is now actually working with the Gastro Doctor in her department (he is overseeing her case as well).*
>
> *So we have our sedatives and continue forward another 24 hours. Your outpouring of love, thoughts, and hosts of prayers mean more to us than you can possibly realize.*
>
> *Love to all, Bonnie*

Thursday and Friday held no new information for us. The slide had been sent to Washington and was very hard to read. This heavy cloud hung over our family all week. We started to focus on getting Jennie to a liver specialist in Tulsa. Bonnie had a phone visit with Dr. Reinhard, Jennie's primary doctor. Bonnie reported:

> *I just talked to Dr. Reinhard. She was very understanding. However, she said at this point to go to a liver specialist in Tulsa would not get us anywhere. I asked if we should do more tests at this point—if they are having that much difficulty reading it, if we will have confidence in the result. She just said she will call Dr. Casner and get back with us.*

We got a tentative diagnosis from the Pathologist, Dr. Casner on Friday, April 9, 2010. The diagnosis was a *low grade vascular neoplasm*. We set up a tentative appointment with Dr. DeLo at the Bartlesville Cancer Center for the next week. But we never made it that far.

That Friday evening, Bonnie's sister Jenarold and her dad, whom we affectionately call "Baba," came over to the house to sit with us. Jennie was feeling good enough to Skype with Robb, who had returned to Seoul, South Korea to take a new teaching job. He had been at the new school for one week. Robb was able to take us on a "laptop tour" of his apartment and of the streets of Seoul just outside his apartment window. He loved his job and the people he was working with. Of course, they had already fallen in love with him, too.

Around 9 p.m., Jenarold and Baba said goodnight and left. As we were getting ready for bed, I heard Bonnie call out that Jennie was hurting. I came out of our bedroom to see Jennie writhe in pain, standing in the doorway to the living room. She bent over. "Daddy," she cried out, "it hurts so badly!" That moment would come back to haunt me numerous times in the months ahead and still can bring tears to my eyes. One of the worst feelings a parent can have is to see your child suffering and not be able to do anything about it.

Bonnie and I rushed Jennie to the Emergency Room at Jane Phillips Medical Center. That night is a blur to me. I know that Bonnie stayed by Jennie's side all night long while I paced the floor. Bonnie captured it best when she emailed her friends:

> *Went to the ER at midnight—Jen screaming in pain. Admitted her at 5:30 a.m. Saturday. We met with Dr.*

> *DeLo, the oncologist, about 1: 30. Sarcoma. Liver filled throughout. Not viable for surgery or transplant. Chemo is our only option. Have a lot of family around and that helps. Jen is being very brave.*

When Dr. DeLo came into our room, he sat down and calmly explained Jennie's condition to us. I remember he would begin each answer to our questions with the word, "Unfortunately." Unfortunately, Jennie had already had the lifetime limit of Adriamycin, the most effective weapon in his chemo arsenal. Unfortunately, radiation and surgery were not options. Unfortunately, people with this severe of the disease could expect to live seven months at the most. Unfortunately, the only chemotherapy they could use had only a 50% chance of having any effect at all.

Unfortunately, there was no hope for survival.

When Dr. DeLo left the room that Saturday, Jennie looked at me and cried out, "Daddy, you said it wouldn't be cancer! I don't want to die! I don't want to die!"

I grabbed her and held her tight and told her how sorry I was that I was wrong. Bonnie, Jennie and I wept uncontrollably. My mind flashed back to the day I carried Jennie out of that last chemotherapy treatment in June 1984. The oncologist told us that we had every reason to believe that Jennie would never face cancer again. How could we be facing cancer again? How could there be no medical hope? Maybe we could get to M.D. Anderson Medical Center and find a specialist who could work a miracle! The only other option was to fly immediately to California where there was experimental testing going on. Although a trip like that would have been logistically impossible anyway, Jennie was ruled out as a candidate because of the severity of her condition.

Our family had to face the fact that the radiation treatments that saved Jennie's life in 1982 had caused a secondary cancer of the liver that would end her life. Maybe we had seven months. Just maybe. I slipped away to the fifth floor waiting room to cry. I have never cried so hard in my life. My brother-in-law, Stan Mullins, came into the waiting room and sat beside me. There is nothing that can be said to make things better. Stan did all that anyone could do: he was there for me.

Although I tried to compose myself before I returned to Jennie's room, Jennie noticed immediately that I had been crying. She looked at me and said, "Oh, Daddy don't cry!

I don't want you and Momma to cry! Let me pray for you!" She was always extremely shy about praying out loud. She would wave off the opportunity if we were at a meal. She just wasn't comfortable with it. But now, in a moment I will also never forget, my daughter prayed the most beautiful prayer for me. She never once asked for healing. She just prayed for God's comfort in my life and the life of her mom and brother. I tried so hard to be strong for Jennie, but here she was being amazingly strong for me. She gave me a hug. Have you ever heard an angel pray? I have!

By Sunday morning, Jennie's condition was getting worse. Dr. DeLo reported to us that Jennie's kidneys were shutting down. This was a definite sign that we may have as little as one day left. Bonnie began a desperate attempt to get Jennie admitted to M.D. Anderson Medical Center as soon as possible.

Our District Superintendent, Dave McKellips and his wife, Gloria came by on Sunday evening. He gave a report to the District family by writing:

> *. . . The news today was not encouraging. Jennie has been diagnosed with malignant sarcoma. The tumor has enveloped the liver . . . The tumor is not operable, or amenable to radiation therapy . . . Please keep Jennie and her family in your prayers! They need a miracle . . .*

I remember meeting Bonnie in a hallway of the hospital. She said, "I can't believe this is happening again! I don't think I can do it." We held each other and cried. My wife is one of the most amazing people in the world, with tremendous emotional strength when forced to deal with severe problems. Her strength was about to be tested to the limit.

When God's Silence is Deafening

GROWING UP IN a Christian home and in the Church, I have a pretty good education when it comes to the subject of prayer. God has used a number of people as my teachers along the way.

My parents, Don and Millie Schuneman, taught me both *how* to pray and *when* to pray.

When it was my turn to pray for a meal, I could recite, "*God is great, God is good . . .*" without even breaking a sweat. At bedtime, I first learned the children's prayer, "Now I lay me down to sleep . . ." Of course, that phrase "if I die before I wake" may explain why I always had trouble with insomnia—if I was always awake, there could be no dying beforehand. I was always tired, but at least I did not die in my sleep.

Learning to pray was *fun* too! For family devotions, we would all kneel in the living room. Usually, Dad or Mom would pray. I must admit I did not always have my mind focused on their words, because I was preparing to pounce on my Dad's back before he could get up. I always got to go on a "horsey back" ride after prayer time. I would jump on his back before he could stand, then he would crawl around the floor on all fours until he got tired. I was greatly saddened when this tradition stopped. Of course, I guess a sixteen-year-old might be too heavy.

In Sunday School, I learned *what* prayer was. The formal definition I learned was that prayer is "talking to God." I came to understand that it is possible to stop anywhere in the world in order to tell God your problems. I had no problem talking to God at school before a test or when I got grass stains on my white pants ("Mom, I was walking down the street when this yard grabbed me and threw me down"). If God loved me, surely He would want to hear all my circumstances and *fix* them.

Evangelists taught me *how long* a person is supposed to pray. An hour a day is the acceptable length of time to satisfy God's standard of successful praying. This cannot be six ten-minute sessions, but one continuous solid hour. I was actually glad to find out the specifics on the question of length of prayer time. It kept me from continuing to go the altar every time an evangelist opened the altar for those who had not prayed enough. I do not remember praying for an hour a day, but at least I knew what the goal was. I could rationalize with God from there.

Dynamics for Discipleship taught me that prayer is *not just about petitioning God's help,* but should include *praising* Him for who He is, *thanking* Him for what He has done and *interceding* for someone else. This lesson gave a more proper perspective than my "Give me, God!" approach I once had. This four-dimensional prayer approach did make my prayer life more enjoyable.

God Himself taught me that prayer is *God talking to me.* During the time of Jennie's first cancer, God spoke to me in the two dreams I had in 1982, telling me that Jennie's malignant cancer would be curable. But He also talked to me when I was wide awake, like at stop lights near the hospital and throughout numerous hospital visits. This was not a hard transition for two reasons: First, I needed Him to talk to me desperately. Second, I had always talked to myself anyway, so if God wanted to join in, I was fine with that.

It was during this time that I learned how prayer and preaching are tied together. Before, I worked really hard to get ten to twelve pages of notes and outlines. Now, suddenly, I didn't have time to prepare notes at all, or even find three words that started with the same letter. I found myself sharing what God had been teaching me through the challenges of the week. One Sunday, I even decided to preach without notes. A new young couple sat on the front row on the edge of their seats. They greeted me at the door by saying, "We'll be back! We've never heard anyone preach without notes before." I hardly ever used notes from that time forward.

From a video prayer seminar by Glaphre Gilliland, I learned that prayer is also *listening to God.* Prayer is a two-way street. It is me talking to God *and* God talking to me. How many times did I ask for God's direction, but not give Him time to give me His solutions. The seminar helped me combine my understanding of prayer as me talking to God with my experience of God talking to me. I learned to listen for God's Voice wherever I was.

The hardest lesson I have ever learned about prayer is that sometimes *God is silent!* I am not talking about those "dry times" in our life when God seems a million miles away. I certainly have experienced those times in my life. They always pass. I am talking about prayer including a time when you know God understands your desperate need, you know He hears you, but He intentionally is not talking to you. That Silence can be deafening!

When we were waiting for news on Jennie's first cancer, God spoke to me so clearly that no one could talk me out of knowing that I was hearing God's voice. I clung to the two dreams and every *Word* He spoke to me. Every time we were in the hospital, He reminded me that His Promise for Jennie was still true. I loved the assurance that His small whisper could bring.

During the week of waiting that followed Jennie's first CT scan; I kept listening for God to say, "It is all going to be fine." Instead: silence! The doctor came to give us the initial results of the CT scan. He reported, "Part of the liver looks dead." Silence! On Saturday, the oncologist came in to confirm it was liver cancer. Silence! When he told us we were looking at seven months at the most, silence! I had talked to Him. I had listened for Him. I am sure I did more than one hour of prayer. Silence!

Why did not God step into the hospital room and announce with great confidence, "Man's answer is that nothing can be done, but with God all things are possible"? Years ago, I heard a testimony of a man whose liver was so diseased that it "broke off" during surgery. The doctors sent him to a nursing home to die. One night during what was supposed to be his last days, he woke up starving for food. The staff found him devouring everything in the home's kitchen. He went to the surgeon who had given up all hope and was pronounced cured of the cancer. God, why not perform another miracle in Jennie's life? Speak to me! Say something!

Silence.

Why would God remain silent when I so desperately needed Him to talk to me? It was little comfort to me that His silence could be interpreted as God being honest with me: Jennie was going to die. I was not ready to hear that God was silent because He was suffering with me. I can believe that is true, but I did not want to hear it while my daughter's life hung in the balance. "God, remember this is Jennie. You do remember her, right? Beautiful, little curly-headed girl with the Angel Kiss you gave her. Surely, you have another miracle in store for us. Go ahead; just give me a detail or two."

Silence.

As much as I tried to force words in to God's mouth, not a word was spoken. By that first Sunday at Jane Phillips Medical Center, I resigned myself to the fact that the doctor's report was correct. My daughter had only hours to live. My brother-in-law, Stan Mullins, took me out to eat at

Outlaws that Sunday. I excused myself and went outside to sit down and cry. I made a desperate call to my friend, Dave Clark. I needed to tell somebody. I am sure he did not understand anything else I muttered, but I was calling him to see if he could write a song for Jennie's funeral. I wanted my friends Randy Phillips, Shawn Craig and Dan Dean to sing it. I knew Dave could write an amazing song in two days. Dave had done songs in minutes. All I communicated to Dave was that Jennie had been diagnosed with terminal cancer and was going to die within a couple of days. He was shocked! He did everything he could to try to comfort me.

When I hung up the phone, the Pastor of one of the Baptist churches came out of the restaurant. When he saw my obvious tears, he approached me and said, "Randy, what's wrong?" I told him, "I just found out that my daughter is dying." He comforted me and prayed for me. I calmed down for a little bit.

Stan drove us back to the hospital parking lot. Before I got out of the car, I called Stumpf Funeral Home to make arrangements for Jennie's funeral. I am not sure that Margaret at Stumpf's understood what I was saying through my tears. Usually, people wait until the person has died to call the funeral home.

I did not like it, but I was resigned to the reality of Jennie's impending death. I fully expected her to die by the next day. If God's silence meant He was preparing me for Jennie's death, I would be strong for Bonnie and Jennie. Even with a broken heart, I needed to be "the Man" of the family. Step up, Schuneman! Get your act together!

When the "good" news came that some of Jennie's pain was caused by excess fluid from the three CT scans she underwent, I began to have a glimmer of hope. Do you know what it feels like to go from utter despair to a glimmer of hope? Maybe I had misunderstood God's silence! Maybe He was trying to keep a miraculous secret from me! I was okay with that.

Over the next two and a half months that Jennie lived, there were moments of laughter and joy, but never once a "strong Word" from the Lord. Just silence. Was God just being mean? Did He give us that hope just to crush us again?

I want to tell you how this story concluded with a "fairy tale" ending. How there was a miraculous healing followed by an amazing celebration and a world-wide tour of Jennie testifying how God had healed her twice. But this did not happen. I would at least like to tell you how God sent His Holy Spirit to explain why all these events ended in Jennie's death, but that didn't happen either.

85

The hardest lesson I have ever learned about prayer is that it includes times when God is silent. He is in the room with you, but not saying a word. There are times when God allows His children to go through circumstances that have no explanation. They make no sense!

It is nothing like losing one job only to end up with a much better job. It is not getting money in the mail the same day a bill was due.

I found no solace when people said things like, "God always has a purpose for everything" or quoted Romans 8:28, which says that "all things work together for good for those who love the Lord." What is the purpose of a young woman dying of liver cancer? What is "good" about that? How do you take those circumstances and "work them together" until a bad thing becomes good?

As I struggled with making sense out of Romans 8:28, I read Romans 8:29. This didn't solve all my problems, but Romans 8:29 explains that the "good thing" God does with our lives is "*conform us* to the image of His Son." A part of my walk with God is to understand that He must remain silent at times in order for us to experience the depths of His heart. The Good is being like him. Not unexpected gifts or acing a test or winning a date with your "dream girl." This Good hurts! Being like Jesus is not only about miracles and blessings. It is also about allowing God to break our hearts more deeply than we could ever imagine so that we can better understand how deep His sorrow goes. God is still God when life does not make sense.

Still, I am laughing again. I love listening to music again. On occasion, I even like to dance (in the privacy of my own home). However, I will never minister to a family that has lost a loved one in the same manner that I used to. While God was being silent, He allowed me to feel the hurt that death brings. I never understood the tears or the loneliness or the emptiness of death until I experienced it first-hand. Strangely enough, I am a better pastor now that I am not a Pastor. The funeral may be well-planned and well-executed, but that is only the beginning of the pain. I now realize that the follow-up ministry to someone who is grieving is as important as the funeral itself.

I cannot explain the loss of my daughter as a "good thing." I never will be able to do that, but I can tell you that through all the pain and heartache, there has been a "conforming to the image of His Son" that has taken place in my heart. The comfort that I have found is in releasing the "need to understand." God does hurt with us! It is hard for Him to remain silent! It is okay to trust Him when what has happened does not make a lick of sense! My relationship with Christ includes giving Him the permission to be silent.

We are very uncomfortable with silence in our culture. Silence makes us nervous. It seems we are always in the midst of "noise" of some kind. Our iPods blare, our Facebook page must be "speaking" to our friends about the fact we brushed our teeth this morning or have entered an "it's complicated" relationship. Our large-screen televisions must be on whether or not we're home. We try to avoid silence at all cost.

For me, silence has been an evidence of my shyness. However, it has also been evidence that I am comfortable with the person I am with. I do not have to impress them with my constant chatter. Just *being with* the ones I love is enough for me sometimes. I am becoming more and more at peace with the Silence of God. God is still God whether He is speaking the universe into existence or becoming the Word in Bethlehem or silently waiting beside us when we do not understand.

Does that answer all my questions? Absolutely not! Does that bring closure to my pain? Not for a moment! This wound will always be open, but there will be healing as I become a changed person. The best vessel in God's hands is a broken one.

The Talk

IT FELT LIKE the closing scene of the movie *Brian's Song*. Gayle Sayers (Billy Dee Williams) stands by the bedside of his dying friend, Brian Piccolo (James Caan) for one final conversation. These two men have become like brothers during their time as roommates on the Chicago Bears. Sayers is a future Hall of Famer. Piccolo will make his greatest impact off the football field. As death approaches, their conversation turns to the deepest issues of the heart. The men talk as if this may be their last conversation, and it is! They are not afraid to cry or say, "I love you." Honesty and transparency become the first priority.

In my situation, I thought surely, this was not really happening. It felt surreal to be in this position. No father ever wants to have this conversation, but as difficult as it was, I will always cherish this sacred moment as a gift from God. Jennie's hospital room became a "Holy of Holies" for the two of us. When I stepped through the door, her twin cousins, Mindy and Cindy were visiting with her. When I took a seat beside Jennie's bed, the girls quietly stepped outside. I found myself alone with Jennie for the first time since we had been told the unbelievable news. It had been a week since we got the prognosis. Our minds had been spinning as we tried to get our heads around the life-changing information. Now, as if God had ordained it, I sat alone with my daughter.

What do you say to someone you love so deeply when you know that the time remaining is being measured in days or weeks? The temptation is to avoid the issue of death altogether, as if that will make it go away. Surely, it is possible to deny the facts into non-existence. My personal advice to anyone who is facing the loss of a loved one is seize those moments when you can communicate from your heart. You will never regret telling someone how much you love them, but you will regret not doing it enough.

Jennie broke our awkward silence. She said, "Daddy, I have been thinking. I have all this money in my retirement funds. I think I'll withdraw it all and spend every last dime before I die. I can buy whatever I want, a new car or television—whatever my heart desires! What do you think?"

We both laughed, because above all else, Jennie was very tight with her money. Every penny she earned was carefully accounted for. Major and minor financial decisions were made only after extensive research and contemplation. I had been trying to convince Jennie to get a new TV. She had the money, but evaluated whether she *needed* it or just *wanted* one. The idea of "shooting the wad" was totally foreign to Jennie's thinking. Now, she enjoyed the thought that she could buy a new television and a new car—with cash.

My voice broke as I responded to Jennie's comments, "Baby girl, I cannot imagine what life will be like without you. You are such an important part of us. We love you so much!" Our laughter was quickly replaced with tears.

Jennie responded, "Daddy, I worry about you, Mom and Robbie. I need to know that you can take care of yourselves."

I said, "Jennie, we need to worry about you right now. We will handle it when the time comes."

Jennie continued, "Still, there are some things that I can only tell you right now. When I tell Mom, she thinks I am giving up. But I'm not quitting. I just don't want to go through all the needle sticks or the sickness of chemotherapy if there is no hope of getting better."

She continued, "When the doctor came to talk to us the first time, he said my chances were '50-50.' I thought he meant I had a 50% chance of being cured. I now realize that he meant there was a 50% chance that treatment would make any difference at all. I am not giving up, but I don't want to go to the medical center in Houston. If I have to die, I want to stay here where I can see my family and all my friends from work."

We talked about the freedom Jennie now had to tell people exactly what was on her heart. If her friends were estranged from their family, she could tell them how important it was for them to seek reconciliation. She could be honest when talking about God with her friends. They loved her too much to argue. During those two weeks, talking about God became a natural part of every conversation Jennie had.

All of her life, Jennie had dreamed of being married. She did not date in high school or college, but as she got older, she focused on finding "Mr. Right." She dated a couple of matches from eHarmony, an online dating service, but nothing worked out. What amazed me most was when Jennie said, "Daddy, I understand now why God didn't allow me to get married. If He had, I would have a husband and two children that would be grieving right now. I would have hated to watch them suffer."

We also talked about being able to see Gammy (Bonnie's Mom, Bernice) again. She would be able to see all of her "cancer kids" that had died in the last seven years. Jennie's smile came back with a courage that only a "saint" could have. She even told me, "I am so glad for the twenty-six extra years that God gave our family to be together." I would have had a difficult time hearing that from someone else, but somehow from her lips, it sounded right.

When we finished "The Talk," I prayed for my daughter. At one point, I prayed, "Thank you, Lord for the joy that Jennie brought into our lives."

Without looking up, Jennie said, "Present tense, Daddy. Never speak about me in past tense."

I corrected my prayer by saying, "Thank you, Lord for the joy that Jennie brings into our lives."

Jennie said, "That's better!"

I noticed that Jennie's tears had dried up. With a maturity far beyond her years, Jennie began to talk about facing death with a determination to make her last days count. She had things to do and people to see. That goal was reached in amazing proportions. Every day, nurses, doctors and other personnel from throughout the hospital would "stream" through Jennie's room. Because Jennie had been a PICC nurse, she had traveled throughout the hospital. Although they may not have known her name, everybody knew the perky girl with the funny blue bonnet on. I saw a whole hospital moved by Jennie's condition. When Jennie was out of her room, there was always a "gang" of people standing around her to find out how she was doing.

One of those special visitors was a doctor Jennie worked with. Although Dr. V. was always good to Jennie, he was not known to be "warm and fuzzy." The day after "The Talk," Jennie's head nurse and a co-worker came to make their daily visit.

They both said, "I wouldn't be surprised if Dr. V. comes to see you soon. He asked about you yesterday, but I guess we did not give him enough information. He asked even more questions today. It is not like him to make a personal visit to anyone other than his patients, but do not be surprised if he comes around."

On Tuesday, two days after "the Talk," the floor nurse came into Jennie's room and announced with great excitement, "There is a man here to see you!"

Jennie responded by asking, "Is he married?"

The nurse replied, "Yes, he is, but he really wants to see you."

Jennie said, "Okay."

There should have been a drumroll when Dr. V. walked into the room! I knew two things about him. First, he had done cancer surgery on a friend of mine; and second, he was building a new home which was being constructed by another friend of mine. I had actually been "in" his house for a walk through a few months before.

The third thing I quickly discovered was that Dr. V. can indeed be "warm and fuzzy." In three months, Jennie had impacted Dr. V.'s life so much that he had to come see her. Jennie and Dr. V. started talking like old high school friends. Jennie asked about what had been happening in the endoscopy department that day. They both laughed and kidded with each other. They bantered back and forth as if they were family.

I nearly fell to the floor when Jennie said, "Dr. V., this is my Dad. He knows how bad my condition is. We have even had "The Talk." Not "THE talk," but the one about dying. Dad, we never had THE talk. Why didn't you tell me about "the birds and the bees?"

I quickly answered, "You never asked!"

About fifteen minutes into the visit, Dr. V. got a call on his cell phone. He listened and then responded, "I understand. I will be there in a moment." Then he continued to talk to Jennie for another fifteen minutes.

The second part of the conversation turned more serious. Just so we knew we had tried our best, we were trying to get Jennie down to M.D. Anderson Medical Center in Houston, Texas. Dr. V. shared a short "lecture" on things to do and not do while at M.D. Anderson.

Like a loving parent, Dr. V. began, "Now, when you get to Houston, make sure that when a doctor comes in your room, you have a family member get between the doctor and the door. If you don't, the doctors and their residents will be in and out of your room without talking to you. They are a teaching hospital. To them, you will just be a number. Don't let them get out of your room until you have all of your questions asked and answered."

Dr. V.'s visit was the talk on the floor for the rest of the week. As a father, I could not help but be overwhelmed how my "little girl" had touched so many lives. Jennie had quietly been the "presence of Jesus" to people at all levels of the hospital. As I watched her for two weeks, I learned that Jennie deeply touched more people than some people do in a lifetime.

For Bonnie, "The Talk" took place during Jennie's stay in Houston. I don't know all the topics that were discussed, but Jennie came back to her room and said, "Daddy, Mom and I talked about seeing Gammy. I don't mean to hurt your feelings, but I am getting excited about seeing her again, and my cancer kids."

For Robb, "The Talk" was more like an ongoing conversation with his sister. As soon as he got home from South Korea, Robb began to talk Jennie through every situation. He became her confidante and her cheerleader in times that were too difficult for me to handle. I saw the depth of character that my son has and the depth of love he has for his sister. Once Jennie came home for good, Robb was by her side both day and night. No one could have asked for a better protector.

Having "The Talk" did not take the pain away, but it is a source of comfort and closure to know that *all hearts are clear.* I am so thankful for our conversation, because the time when Jennie was unable to communicate came very suddenly. There would have been no time had I waited any longer.

Red-Toed Elephants and
Pink Fingernails

WHEN I WAS a teenager, an evangelist came to hold a revival at our church. On the first night of the revival, he handed out little red stick-on dots. We were asked to place the dots on the center of our watches as a reminder to pray for the revival services. Every time you checked your watch, you were to pray for the revival. I still remember seeing that dot on my Timex watch.

One morning, I almost ran over the fifth-floor head nurse. As I stepped off the elevator, she was coming out of her office two steps away. After I apologized, the nurse asked how Jennie was doing. That began a conversation that lasted about 45 minutes! I talked in detail about how God had worked in Jennie's life when she was a child. I think I must have covered 28 years in detail. I apologized for taking so much time, but the nurse wanted to hear more of the story.

At one point in the conversation, I talked about how Jennie had awakened from a dream, looked at Bonnie and said, "Mom, I just had a dream about a red-toed elephant."

While we talked about ways to remind people to pray for Jennie, the nurse's eyes lit up.

She said, "What if everyone in the hospital painted their fingernails red?" I thought it was a great idea, but how could someone get people to cooperate? A few minutes later, the nurse walked by me with bottles of the most neon pink fingernail polish I have ever seen! She walked up to the fifth-floor desk and *commanded* her nurses to begin painting their fingernails pink. Who wants to upset the person who sets the work schedule? They complied!

I would have been pleased if the process had stopped there, but the idea caught on. Before we knew it, nurses from several of the floors were *pink-nailed*. Word got back to the church about this prayer reminder. I am sure that Bartlesville sold out of that shade of pink fingernail polish before it was all over.

The first obstacle that we encountered was with men. You do not have to be a brain surgeon to realize men have a tendency to shy away from fingernail polish altogether, but they will run away from hot pink polish. A settlement was finally ironed out which asked men to paint their right thumb only. One man would only allow his toes to be painted, but his daughter had more fun painting his toes than she would have had with just his fingers.

I was okay with the one-thumb only policy because at first I had someone paint all ten of my fingernails. Jennie did all ten. I thought it was a good idea. It was not. My hands took on a life of their own! I got stares from people who walked by me as if I was a leper. Men, please do not try this at home. My hands were making people nervous. My hands began making *me* nervous. I did not mind being told I looked like my Father, but looking like Mom was not my goal. Jennie finally agreed to let me cut down to my right thumb.

People would come into Jennie's room and display their fingernails as a reminder that they were praying for her. Painting his thumbnail was one of the first things Robb had to do when he returned from South Korea. Uncle Stan and Baba were no exceptions, either. Hot pink nails started showing up everywhere!

I was teaching a Pastoral Care class at Oklahoma Wesleyan University at the time. My students were to meet me in the lobby for a class on hospital visits. I forgot all about it. I had asked Charlie Taraboletti, a friend and a radio announcer, to meet me at the hospital for the purpose of telling Jennie's story. I kept Charlie for two hours! When the students arrived at the hospital, someone escorted them up to fifth floor. While I was talking to Charlie, I had the students go in to meet Jennie and get their fingernails polished.

The visit proved to be one of the best decisions I *never* made! Hillary Boyce, a great family friend and fellow nurse, was in the room with Jennie. The two nurses talked to the class about things *not* to do when making a hospital call. They shared a nurse's perspective on hospital ministry by sharing the *do's* and *don'ts* they had learned from watching ministers.

The students came out with two experiences: a great *lecture* and a hot pink fingernail.

I am sure that some people went home and took the polish off, but I was amazed at how many people *wore* it off. The exercise did what it was supposed to do—remind people to pray for the young woman in room 591.

Show Me the Money!

THE TITLE THAT I have chosen for this chapter comes from the movie *Jerry McGuire*. The movie focuses on the materialistic desires of an NFL football player (Cuba Gooding Jr.). What if you needed to ask God, "Show me the money"—not out of want, but out of a desperate need? How would God respond?

Right before Jennie got sick, Robb moved back to Seoul, South Korea to take another teaching job. In fact, he had only been at his new job for a week when he got the news. Using Facebook, I tried to keep our friends aware of Jennie's condition. One night at dinner while Jennie was in the hospital, my niece asked, "You didn't put anything on Facebook that Robbie would read, did you?" I realized how big a mistake I had made. As soon as I could get to the hospital, I had to tell Jennie that we must let Robbie know. Although we could not reach Robb by phone, we could chat with him through the Internet him using Skype.

I will never forget Jennie setting up the connection, then looking at me and saying, "Daddy, you are going to have to tell him. I don't think I can." Using Jennie's laptop, we got to see Robb's face as I began to tell him the bad news. As soon as I began to talk, Jennie reached out for her laptop and gently turned it towards her face. The news was hard enough to process when we were at the hospital. Imagine how difficult it would be to find out that your sister is dying when you are thousands of miles away.

I stumbled over my words when I first started. Jennie just said, "Bubba, I need you to come home. I am very sick and I need you here."

Trying to let her words sink in, Robb said, "You mean I need to come home today? I don't understand. Are you okay? Jennie answered, "I am stable for now, but . . . I am stable right now. I just need you to come home as soon as possible."

Even though Robb had been at his new school for just one week, the students and faculty loved him already. How do you tell the administrator that you have to leave so soon? How do you get money for airfare home? Do I pack as if I am coming back or totally leaving? All these questions plus a myriad more confronted Robb. It was late when we called. Early the next morning, Robb began the process of making his way home.

When Robb told the administrator his situation, she said, "I'm so sorry. I know you're telling the truth, but the last American teacher left suddenly. We told the students that he had lost his mother. We cannot tell them that you are now going home because your sister is dying."

Not only could they not hold his job, but they had to be reimbursed for the airfare they had spent on Robb before they could allow him to leave the country.

The next day, Robb called and said calmly, "Dad, I need $1,000 in the next few hours so I can pay the school back and fly home. They won't let me leave until then."

Have I mentioned that, unlike my son, I am not laid-back when it comes to stressful situations? Fortunately, I had $1,000 in my checking account, but the banks were closed. Where do you get $1,000 cash when the bank is closed and the clock is ticking? Our great friends, Doc and Marie Livingston were there when we got the call. Doc and I dashed towards his car while brainstorming about how to find the money. As we ran through the hospital foyer, I remembered there was an ATM machine near the stairway to the cafeteria.

Show me the money, I thought to myself. I had never been able to get more than $300 per day from an ATM, but I was desperate. As the money came out, I handed it to Doc to hold onto. Two hundred . . . couldn't hurt to try for four hundred . . . four hundred . . . how about six hundred . . . six hundred . . . luck, don't leave me now . . . *show me the money*, but eight hundred . . . eight hundred . . . might as well go all the way, one thousand . . .the last two hundred dollars came out of the machine. I would dare anyone to find a person who has gotten that much money from an ATM on one day. When I told one of the ladies at the bank, she told me that had never happened before. God does work in mysterious ways.

Now we have $1,000 in cash, but how do you get that to South Korea in a matter of hours? Of course: Western Union! But where is a Western Union location in Bartlesville, Oklahoma? Doc reminded me that there was one inside the grocery store where I shopped. He even knew a cashier named John who could help us.

One of the things that soon came into play is the fact that Doc drove a Chevy convertible pickup. It is one fast machine. As we approached the car, Doc asked, "Do you want the top up or down?" Because I was holding one thousand dollars' worth of twenty dollar bills in my hand along with some vital information, I asked to keep it down. Unfortunately, my dear friend is a little hard of hearing. As soon as we got in the car, the top started going back while the engine revved up. We ended up tearing around like we were in a NASCAR race. If the police stop us, how am I going to explain the cash in my hand? All the time I am thinking, "God, please don't let this money fly out of my hands."

When we got to the store, Doc and I hurried to the counter and there was John. I gave him the school's routing number, which Robb had given me. John told me, "We can't send money to a routing number. We have to send it to a person." No problem! Just send the money to a Western Union in Seoul, South Korea! That would cost $34. I only had one thousand dollars even. What do you do? I used my debit card! So we sent the money in a matter of seconds.

Do you know how many Western Unions locations there are in Seoul, South Korea? I called Robb and proudly told him that his money was waiting for him at the closest Western Union. Robb answered, "Dad, I don't know where a Western Union location is. This is a city of ten million people."

To the untrained eye, everywhere in Seoul, South Korea looks the same. There are no street signs. The stores are in multi-level buildings with the name of the store displayed in Korean on banners outside the floor where the store is located. I panicked. I had just sent $1,000 into cyberspace! I could picture Robb in a Korean prison being fed nothing but rice while he waited on that money to arrive. Robb was pretty certain he could locate the money through the Internet. What I did not hear him say was, "If I miss this flight, I can catch another one tomorrow." Very important information!

As far as I knew, Robb was going to be in late the next day. With anxious thoughts of how badly my son needed my help, I went home, took an Ambien and tried to sleep. The next thing I remember, it was 3 o'clock in the morning and I was talking to my friend Steve Boyce on the phone. I was sitting at my computer; he was at work at a General Motors plant. Steve has always been our "go-to guy" for good travel deals. I didn't think it strange to be talking to Steve about getting the best deal. But after an hour, I remember thinking it was strange that Steve would call me so late, and then be impatient with *me*. Finally, at about four in the morning, Steve said, "Robbie has already taken care of it. He booked his flight for tomorrow. Good night, Randy."

Two questions came to mind. First, why did Steve call me so late? Second, why did he call me from work? I could hardly hear him over the noise at the truck plant. Steve was talking to me while talking to several airlines about prices while giving orders to his guys at the factory. Even so, I fell asleep immediately after Steve said, "Good night, Randy." Like a rock, I passed out in my computer chair. I am still not sure how I ended up in bed.

I called Steve back the next day. I had to ask him, "Did I call you or did you call me?" He said, "Randy, you called me. I couldn't get you off the phone! Robb is coming home tomorrow night." I learned then that Ambien does have a side effect of temporary amnesia. You can eat three bowls of cereal and not remember it in the morning. You can also call good friends without knowing how you dialed their number.

We made a big deal of greeting Robb at the airport the next day. Little did we know how much we would need his quiet strength in the days that lay ahead.

That Goes in the Book

JENNIE GOT HER good looks and organizational skills from Bonnie. However, she got her sense of humor from me. Our family has a corporate sense of humor. All four of us can break out in song when a certain word or lyric is used. For example, when we hear a meteorologist say that it's going to be sunny tomorrow, we may simultaneously break into "The Sun Will Come Out Tomorrow" from the Broadway show, *Annie.* If it is someone's birthday, we could sing a barbershop quartet version of "Oh Happy Birthday to You!" That is the birthday song we used in Sunday School opening when I was growing up.

And our family loves to play table games. Although we are competitive, we usually are laughing most of the time we play. We play a card game (with *Rook cards*, Mom) called *Sabotage.* Without explaining all the rules, just know that someone always loses badly. While the winner may score 140 points, someone else will end up with only 30. When the final score is read, someone will add, "Have you ever noticed that there is always a player that finishes WAY behind the rest?" Maybe you had to be there.

On our long trips home from Michigan, we would laugh as we played the *Alphabet Game* where you try to find the alphabet from A to Z on the signs you drive past or the *License Plate Game* where you tried to see how many states were represented by the cars around.

While we have a corporate sense of humor, we all have our own individual *styles.* Although Bonnie can be hilarious, most of the time, I am her stand-up comic. One of the many things that drew me to Bonnie was that she *got* my sense of humor. I could make this beautiful young woman laugh! Still today, one of my favorite things is to hear my wife laugh. If it's me that caused her laughter, that's even better.

Robb and I work best together as a comedy team. I usually serve as the *straight man* that sets up the funny line. Robb feeds off whatever I say.

The closest example I can think of is the Smothers Brothers, where Dick was the set-up person. Robb has a vast knowledge of about everything, so it is not hard for him to stay up with me. The only thing that we must steer away from is politics. That topic seems to stop being funny as soon as we get started.

Jennie was my comical clone. It was scary sometimes to realize that the same line would come to us simultaneously. On occasion, it verged on comic telepathy. Our eyes would meet when we knew what the other one was thinking. I can still remember the first joke I ever told, but telling jokes in not my strong suit. What Jennie and I both enjoyed was coming up with a *zinger*—a line or phrase that caught people off guard and made them laugh. Some of her co-workers were trying to set Jennie up on a blind date. After the friends described the man, Jennie responded, "So you are trying to set me up with a leprechaun!"

Jen shared my love for puns. She also shared my disappointment when people either did not hear or did not understand what she said. She would always respond, "That was a good one! Why didn't you all laugh?" When Jennie thought something was funny, she had this contagious laugh you could not miss.

When Jennie started attending church with us in Bartlesville, she became the choir clown. She would say something funny or add an exclamatory sound at the end of a song. Her favorite song to work with was "God is Good, All the Time." She was famous for ending the song with a loud *Woohoo!* While I was preaching, she loved to laugh really loud at a funny comment I made or shout an extra-loud, "Amen!" It was always well-timed, so she always got her laugh.

One of Jennie's trademarks was the ability to remember every lyric of every song she ever heard and every line of some of her favorite movies. She could start anywhere in the movie *Pete's Dragon* and sing the songs, make the sounds that Elliott made and sing "Passamaquoddy" perfectly without getting tongue-tied. She and Robbie both knew all the words to every Monkees song in existence, even "D.W. Washburn." Jennie was especially funny when she tried to sing a Christian song that had a rap breakdown. She would practice it until she had it flawlessly in her mind.

Whenever Jennie was sad or discouraged, my role was to make her laugh. I loved to make her laugh. When Jennie got off work, she would call home to talk to Bonnie. If I picked up the phone first, Jennie would usually say, "Can I talk to Mom?" My usual response was, "What am I, meatloaf?"

I decided to take a different strategy one night so when I picked up the receiver, I answered in my best Mickey Mouse voice (and I do a good Mickey Mouse voice). I said, "Hellooo Jennie, this is your Mother." Although it was silly, it made Jennie laugh her head off. What do you do when something funny works? You use it again and again.

From that point forward, I answered her nightly call with the same response. Sometimes, it was before Bonnie got to the phone. Sometimes, it was after a long, dramatic pause when she knew it was coming. Jennie came to the point that she expected it every night. I could even do it numerous times in the same phone call. I kept it up because she could not keep herself from laughing. At times, she would beg me, "Dad, please don't do it! Please!" Of course, I did it, and she laughed every time!

Jennie was funny, but Jennie on pain killers was *hilarious*. Especially during the two weeks in Jane Phillips Medical Center, she was on a constant roll. Her boss, Kim Betts, and her co-worker, Amy Gustus, came for their nightly visit. Jennie had just come back from some kind of x-ray. While Jennie was away, somebody had given her a children's sticker. They had placed it on her robe. Without missing a beat, Jennie removed the sticker from her gown and slapped it on her forehead and started singing "Prince Ali" from the film *Aladdin*. Apparently, this was not the first time the Endoscopy Department had sung the song. Fortunately, Kim had brought along her video camera. Amy stopped Jennie and then the two of them started from the beginning of the song.

Jennie was heavily medicated, but she sang her heart out. In the middle of the song, Amy said, "I don't remember the rest of the lyrics." Jennie was not bothered a bit. She sang the song all the way to the end without missing one word.

Now, some of you are saying, "Big Deal!" Let me share just a few lines from the song!

> *Prince Ali! Fabulous he!*
> *Ali Ababwa Genuflect, show some respect*
> *Down on one knee!*

> *He's got ninety-five white Persian monkeys (He's got the monkeys, let's see the monkeys) And to view them he charges no fee . . .*

> *Heard your princess was a sight lovely to see*

And that, good people, is why he got dolled up and
dropped by
   With sixty elephants, llamas gators
   With his bears and lions
   A brass band and more
   With his forty fakirs, his cooks, his bakers
   His birds that warble on key
   Make way for Prince Ali!

Just try remembering those lines with morphine in your blood system! It was not long after the song was finished that Jennie was sound asleep. She was so funny that I kept a Styrofoam cup near her bed for tips.

As a PICC nurse—the person who inserts a tube into the vein and through the body up to the heart—Jennie had the reputation of being a good "sticker." If you ever had to have blood drawn or been given a shot, you know that it makes a big difference who handles the needle. With her *cancer kids,* her goal was to administer their chemo without causing any pain. From her own personal experience, she knew how important it was to keep the children's veins useable. When she became a PICC nurse, her biggest task was finding a good vein to use. After diligent work experience, she could spot a vein from across the room. Like a dentist notices teeth, Jennie noticed veins.

During a visit from her Uncle Stan and Aunt Vicky Mullins, a sedated Jennie stopped in the middle of the conversation and said, "Wow, Uncle Stan, you have great veins!" She examined them and then added, "Aunt Vicky, did you marry Uncle Stan because of his veins?"

She was pointing to something on the wall of her room. As she extended her arm to point, her attention was drawn back to the *needle work* done to her arm. Like someone with Attention Deficit Disorder, Jennie said, "Do you see that picture on the wa—Wow! Would you look at how well they placed my needle!"

A PICC nurse came to put a line in for Jennie when she was not heavily sedated. Jennie got all excited. She told Bonnie, "Mom, look! This is what I used to do." Then she began a consult with the nurse helping her find a good vein. Jennie instructed, "Why don't we try that one? It looks like our best option."

Throughout her stay at JPMC, Jennie kept a notebook of funny things she had said. After someone would laugh, she would say, "That goes in the book!" The notebook was pretty full by the time she left the hospital for Houston. What a great treasure!

While we were at M.D. Anderson Cancer Center in Houston, Jennie had one injection of chemotherapy. Jennie went into the chemo room and prepared for her treatment. I had chosen to go in with her, but Jennie looked at me and said, "Mrs. Boyce. I want Mrs. Boyce. Dad, you don't talk enough. I need Mrs. Boyce. Go get her for me. Let's get this thing going!"

When Jennie returned to her home after our time in Houston, a group from the church came to pray for her. Shelley Ingmire, a dear friend and a real cut-up, wheeled Jennie outside as the group joined hands. They prayed and sang an old hymn.

Hymns usually have verses and choruses. Some choruses have counterparts. While the soprano and altos sang the main melody, the basses and tenors would sing different words that went along with the chorus. For instance, the chorus to the hymn

> *Wonderful Grace of Jesus goes,*
> *Wonderful the matchless grace of Jesus,*
> *Deeper than the mighty rolling sea (the rolling sea);*
> *Higher than the mountain, sparkling like a fountain, All*
> *sufficient grace for even me (for even me, sing it);*
> *Broader than the scope of my transgressions,*
> *Greater far than all my sin and shame (my sin and shame);*
> *O magnify the precious Name of Jesus, Praise His Name!*

I looked over at Jennie in her wheelchair with Shelley kneeling beside her. They were singing the counterpart with gusto! When they got to the end of the chorus, they just laughed. Up until the time the final pain started and Jennie could not communicate any more, she found something to smile about through it all.

There was one joke I pulled that would have embarrassed Jennie to death. Thank goodness, she never knew about it. Right before Bonnie got to the hospital to spend the night, Jennie asked me to go find the male nurse who was responsible for her room that night. Let's call him Fred (his real name was Joe, but I cannot let anyone know that). I found Fred out in the hallway. I put my hands on his shoulder, looked him straight in the eye and said, "Fred, my daughter is calling for you. I need to let you in on a little secret: the whole reason Jennie is on this floor tonight is to get closer to you." Jennie was on the fifth floor of JPMC, which is a geriatrics floor. She was extremely sick and not in her right mind.

To my surprise, Fred responded, "Really?" I tried to explain that I was only kidding, but I guess he took me seriously. He quickly went to Jennie's room, stood by her bedside and asked how he could help her.

Now the issue was whether or not Jennie wanted the light above her head on or off. I saw Fred's trembling hand hover over the button for that light waiting for Jennie's response. Because of her medication, Jennie was feeling the weight of the world on her shoulders to make this epic decision. In that instance, I wish Jennie would have seen something she always wanted to experience—a young man shaking over being in her presence.

The final decision was (*drum roll*) off! I thought my dumb little joke was over. However, when Bonnie came to prepare for the night, she usually had to have the hospital chair made out into a bed. These chairs were a little tricky. While we are struggling with the transformation of this contraption, Fred enters the room and immediately takes charge of the chair! He asked if there was *anything* she needed. Please understand why I tell that story. It is not to make fun of Fred. In fact, I would love to thank him for making a Dad's heart full of joy as I watched a dream of Jennie's come true. Someone was in awe of her beauty! She deserved that. Thank you, Fred! It meant the world to me.

I can imagine Jennie standing before Jesus. They're both smiling, maybe even laughing and rejoicing as Jesus says, "Jennifer Dawn Schuneman—now that goes in the Book!"

Let's Party

BONNIE ALWAYS TRIED to make Jennie and Robbie's birthdays something special. Beyond the cake and ice cream and presents, she always tried to make sure that all of the kids' friends were invited. Poor Robb did not know many boys his age when we first moved to Flint. There was a group of fifth and sixth grade boys, though, who volunteered themselves to be Robbie's "homeys" that year. He never forgot that special party. He was four at the time. What a big deal to have so many buddies around him.

For Jennie, birthdays meant slumber parties. Jen was blessed to have a large group of girls her age in the church. All of them would come with their pajamas packed for the night. There was always a lot of giggling and very little sleep. Bonnie and I usually took the next day off to get back on a proper sleep schedule.

There were always gifts to open. I personally made sure that there was at least one gift that was "overdone." I found something that I probably could not afford, because I wanted them to know how much I loved both of them. As I have mentioned, Robbie got autographed memorabilia from his favorite professional players. Bonnie usually got Jennie smaller gifts, focusing on quantity. It did not take much to make Jennie squeal in delight. Crayons, coloring books, pajamas, clothing and a new Disney video would make Jennie's day.

For her first birthday, I dressed up like a clown, wrote a poem entitled "It's Your Birthday, Baby Girl" and knelt down on one knee to read my "masterpiece" to that beautiful, little one-year-old. I looked very silly, but I did not care about looking "manly." I just needed to let my Jennifer know how much I loved her.

We tried to make every birthday something they would never forget. But how do you celebrate what you know will be your child's last birthday? What if you are praying that she will even actually make it to her birthday?

One doctor already said that Jennie should have died the first weekend in the hospital. Her birthday was April 21, 2010. That looked so far away on April 10.

As only my wife could do, Bonnie began to plan for an early birthday party in case Jennie did not live until the 21st. She asked Carolyn Jenner, a good friend and great planner, if she would coordinate a full-blown party extravaganza. Church members and co-workers were secretly invited to hide in one of the larger conference rooms just inside the side door of JPMC. A cake was ordered. A plane ticket was bought for Jennie's great friend, Laura Andrus, who always made Jennie smile. A program was planned that would begin with Laura jumping out of a fake cardboard building when Jennie came in the door.

Buddy Stefanoff made special LED badges for us that flashed the message, "Happy Birthday, Jennie." The signs clipped on with a magnet. He also made Jennie a special LED tiara for Jennie to wear to celebrate her position as "Princess Jennifer."

As Bonnie and Jennie approached, the lights were turned off. The crowd was quieted to a complete hush. Jennie thought that Bonnie was bringing her down to have another visit with Charlie. When the lights flashed on and everyone called out, "Surprise!" Jennie began to cry. Bonnie rolled our daughter a little closer to the front of the room. Out popped Laura. Jennie squealed, "Laura, my Laura!"

When Jennie was in her place as guest of honor, Carson and Terry West began a short program which combined Jennie's love for *Wheel of Fortune* and her desire to go to Hawaii someday. Contestants were chosen to be Jennie's "opponents." Although the contestants tried their hardest, Jennie put them to shame! After all, it was a "prize puzzle!" No one was better at prize puzzles than Jennie. The puzzle had something to do with a "Trip to Hawaii." That is as close as she ever came to fulfilling her dream of going to Hawaii.

While the cake and ice cream were being served, I slipped back to where Buddy and Dana were filming the event. I was in complete denial of the fact that we were losing Jennie. Surely, if God was going to take her, He would have done it the first weekend, I thought. I look back at the pictures of that event and realize how intentionally blind I was to what was going on before my eyes.

Dr. K came back, sat beside me and said, "How is Dad doing?" I fully believed God was going to heal Jennie like before. I said, "I am just fine!" Then, Dr. K started to cry. His son had been severely injured in a car accident. Although he did not die from the accident, his son's life would never be the same. Nor would Dr. K's family.

Dr. K went on, "I knew it had to be bad, really bad when I saw the x-rays." He went on to talk about how much he appreciated and loved Jennie. He would be praying for us. It was hard to believe that Jennie could love and be loved by people she had only met three months before! I moved up behind Jennie and whispered in her ear. After the short program, the party seemed ready to break up. That's when I started to set up a "dance floor." Jennie's weakness, her tears, her eloquent thanks to the group of friends—all of it went over my head. I wanted to dance! God had given my daughter back to me for the second time—I was sure of it!

There is a picture of Jennie and me when she must have been six-months-old. She is sitting up looking towards the camera. I have my back turned away from the camera. All you really notice about me is this long, curly hair (which isn't there anymore!). I am holding her hands.

I love that first picture. However, there was a similar picture taken at the Birthday Party that breaks my heart. The music has started, the crowd is silenced to a "holy hush." I am holding Jennie with my arms wrapped around her. I remember that I am whispering in her ear, "It is going to be all right! I love you so much, Jen!" What I did not see were those tears coming down Jennie's face with this most heartbroken expression on her face. I was trying to hold on, but she knew it was time to start letting go.

Bonnie and Robbie both understood the situation, but I could not see it. Bonnie helped Jennie to sit back in her wheelchair to rest. I wanted to dance across the room. It was going to be just fine! God was in charge! He had done it before. Surely He was going to do it again, right?

And Jennie made it to her actual birthday. The celebration was much quieter than her "Pre-birthday Party." Charlie was more noticeable this time. He roamed the same conference area. We sat and ate a quiet meal together. We ate. We laughed. We hugged. But I wanted to dance! Why couldn't we dance? At that first party, on my makeshift dance floor, *we did dance!* Oh, did we!

The Last Dance

EVER SINCE JENNIE could stand on her own, she loved dancing. All I had to do was clap out a rhythm with some silly melody line and off she would go. Her love for dancing was a life-time characteristic of who she was and is. She had a very large repertoire. There was:

The "circle dance," which consisted of spinning round and round until she got dizzy. Unfortunately, this dance proved to be dangerous at times. We lost one glass lamp and some other fragile items. Jennie did not get hurt, though, or scolded for that matter. How do you discipline an angel for dancing?

The "turkey dance" was a specialty creation that Jennie perfected when she was two. This dance could be done with or without musical accompaniment. Jennie simply put her hands behind her back, leaned over and began walking with a jerking motion. In order for her to perform, you just needed to say, "Jennie, do the turkey dance!" If she had just had feathers, it would have been difficult to tell the difference between the two.

The "line dance" became an important "season" in Jennie's career. The fact that Jennie danced it alone begs the question, "Can you have a line with one person?"

The "Sweatin' to the Oldies dances" were an "on again, off again" element to Jennie's dancing career. When I checked Jennie's iPod library after she died, the Richard Simmons' category was pretty full.

At Christmas, our family had a tradition of dancing to Ricky Martin's, "Ya, ya, ya, it's Christmas!" When the family performed this dance, every family member had their own individual "style." However, Bonnie had to make her cockatoo sound. For the last few years, this dance had become a "solo" performance in which I re-created Tom Cruise's dance in *Risky Business*. Enough said.

Jennie loved all genres of music. No cloud is so dark or day so bad that a little bogeying cannot cure it. One principle always applied, "If there is music, dancing shall break forth." Our family seems to have a "sixth sense" about when dancing should happen. Certain songs send our family into a spontaneous, dancing frenzy. We have a mystical "telepathy" which transcends words. And might I add: *we are good*!

That Jennie was a good dancer is even more amazing when you realize that dancing was a strict taboo in the church we grew up in. However, I speculate that by now there are several "social dancers," if you will, within the Nazarene church. For those people, I say loud and clear, "Hi! My name is Randy Schuneman and I am a social dancer too." Once you confess it, there is an amazing freedom.

Jennie even used her dancing skills on the pediatric oncology floors where she worked. On the day of a child's last day of chemotherapy, Jennie would organize a dance parade. Usually, Jennie would wear her red clown's nose and hold her "marching stick." The children would form a line and do the conga. They would dance down the hallways and back in celebration of the completion of treatment. It did not matter to Jennie how silly she might look, because she knew the feeling of having taken your last chemotherapy shot. Also, few things brought her greater joy than watching children dancing.

The favorite dance for Jennie and me is the "father-daughter waltz." When the time was right, I would put my left arm around Jennie's waist and take her left hand in my right hand. We would float around the room with her doing "twirls" and "spins." Fred Astaire and Ginger Rogers could not have done any better! It was this last dance that played an important role in my saying good-bye to Jennie.

The week before Jennie's surprise "Pre-Birthday Party," I must have rolled over onto my iPod in my sleep, because I woke up to music. Although I had not been listening to the album, the iPod started playing the last two songs on Luther Vandross' Greatest Hits. I woke up to "Here and Now," which is a wedding song. The next song was a cover of Stephen Stills's "Love the One You're With." I realize that the second song would never be sung as a special in church, but Vandross couched the song in a black gospel format. When "Love the One You're With" began to play, I could hardly keep my feet in bed! The bass guitar at the beginning of the song is worth the time to listen.

I did not know what others had planned for the birthday party, but I was bound and determined that Jennie and I were going to dance. On the same Vandross album, there is a song entitled "Dance with My Father." When the short program was over, I said we weren't finished yet. I explained how it had always been Jennie's desire for the two of us to dance at her wedding. Realizing that we would never share that moment, I told the friends there that I wanted to dance with my daughter.

I turned and asked Jennie, "My Lady, may I have this dance?" Jennie replied, "Why, certainly!"

When the music began, I expected to take our normal positions and take a few small steps around her wheelchair. However, when I helped her to her feet, I realized that she was too weak to stand, much less dance. I just held her tightly and whispered how much I loved her. I was too focused on Jennie to hear the crying that was going on in the room. But I hear my own crying now.

Bonnie was concerned about Jennie being too weak. She and Robb joined us in a "group hug" as the song finished its last notes. Everybody in the room understood the poignancy of that moment as they understood the message of that song selection.

However, I am not sure anybody "got" the next song, except Jennie, me and possibly Robb. I called all the little children up to the front so they could join in dancing to "Love the One You're With." I could try to rationalize my theological interpretation of this song that night, but even my wife did not understand. The song started, the bass guitar joined in and the children and I began to do the silliest dance. I looked at Jennie smiling and realized she understood.

Jennie called out, "Conga, Daddy! Do the conga line!" How do you turn down an angel?

I asked the children to follow me. I can still remember my father-in-law (who was 89 at the time) getting up to join in. My former neighbor Larry Barnes, dressed up like Carmen Miranda, fruit and all, also joined the line. I would have to admit we did not have 100% participation, but my heart goes out to those who did. You will never know what it meant for me to see Jennie laughing and clapping.

It was fitting that we played the song "Dancing with the Angels" at Jennie's funeral. We also placed that phrase on her grave marker. In my mind's eye, I can see Jesus giving Jennie a big hug and then breaking out into a "holy jig." When I see Jennie next, I know something we are going to do in the first thousand years is *dance, dance, dance*. Maestro, strike up the band!

Going Home

Jennifer (the Poem)

Who loves playing with kids, going to church,
and spending time with her family.

Who hates driving by semis, being late for anything,
and trying to find her car in the parking lot.

Who cares for her dog, Sassy, her kitten, Opie, and all of her friends.

Who is afraid of driving on the expressway, being late for a
Chorale activity, and killing her brother before he reaches age 15.
Who is curious about life, Heaven, and duck-billed platypuses. Who
values music, baby animals, and the snooze button on her alarm clock.

Who thinks about her future, her loved ones, and
how she can possibly intimidate her brother.

Who is good at playing the piano, writing poetry,
and getting herself into trouble.

Who wonders why people can be so cruel to one another,
why God loves her even when she doesn't deserve it, and
why life always changes before she can get used to it.

Who will someday go to Spring Arbor, have
a family of her own, and travel

Houston, We Have a Problem!

IN ORDER TO know that we had exhausted all resources, the decision was made to take Jennie to M. D. Anderson treatment facility in Houston.

Jennie's first cousin, Cami Mullins, has worked in the Houston area for most of her career. She now works with the seven labs inside of the M.D. Anderson complex. I doubt there are very few people who know the hospital better than Cami does. It was a comfort to know that someone would be waiting to show us around the massive buildings. ConocoPhillips has a program called Angel Flight where patients can fly on the company's jet that makes daily trips from Bartlesville and Ponca City to Houston. We were able to book a flight for Bonnie and Jennie.

When Jennie left the hospital on her way to the local airport, the staff at Jane Phillips formed lines on both sides of the hospital hallway and cheered Jennie on as she left. She left the hospital with the treatment that only movie starts get. Then, it was off on the flight to Houston. Because there was only room for two on the flight, Robb, Bonnie's brother Stan and I headed to Houston by car.

Most of Jennie's initial contacts at M.D. Anderson were on an out-patient basis. Cami's hospitality and positive attitude made our stay at her home a real fun time for Jennie. I do not know if I never noticed before or if it was a new preference, but Jennie fell in love with the color pink. Almost everything that Cami owns is pink! Jennie developed an urgent hunger for pink things. She sent me out to find a pink NIV Bible. This was an uncomfortable assignment for me, but I manned up for it. Pink became Jennie's "color."

Jennie also wanted an autographed copy of one of Max Lucado's older books. You know how to get a Max Lucado autograph? You call his church and ask! Jen got her signed book.

The stay at Cami's would prove to be "the calm before the storm." The waters would be rougher soon! Once we were situated at M.D. Anderson, we met Dr. Ravi, the sarcoma specialist. His nurse came in to greet us. I had a moment of hope when the nurse said, "Dr. Ravi is amazing when it comes to dealing with sarcoma!" But then she added, "Young lady, you have a lot of it."

When Dr. Ravi entered the room, he prepared to show us Jennie's x-rays. I asked if I could step outside. Maybe if I did not see those pictures, I thought, it wouldn't be as bad. I was not ready, emotionally, to handle the bad news. This was our last hope! If M.D. Anderson could not find a cure, we had nowhere else, humanly, to turn.

Unfortunately, I stepped back into the room too early. I saw the x-ray. It was not pretty! The cancer had enveloped most of Jennie's right side. The doctor told us that if the tumors had been above Jennie's shoulders, they would have a better chance of dealing with the cancer. With the tumors located in the liver and other vital organs, Dr. Ravi feared for the worst.

Adriamycin was the "chemo of choice" in this situation. However, Jennie had already taken her life-time amount of the drug. This chemo was no longer an option. Radiation usually was, but Jennie had maxed out on that as well. There was only one option left—this third form of chemo. An appointment was set up for Jennie to receive her first treatment.

I walked Jennie down to the chemo lab as the nurse prepared the drug. I had hardly sat down when Jennie made her request for the more talkative Beth Boyce." The orders were followed, but that proved to be the last thing that went the way we wanted it. The chemotherapy proved ineffective. Jennie quickly got worse.

We were barely able to get her home.

Someone Call Security!

I REALIZE THERE has been much discussion concerning the increased security at US airports since 9/11. Body scanners and intimate body checks have been the focus of the latest concerns. Having someone see your underwear on the body scanner does not bother me that much. If someone is interested in securing a picture of me in my Jockeys, they need help. I do understand the concern about overly thorough body checks. Because someone tried to keep a bomb in his undergarment, we have the privilege of security guards checking places that even we should not touch on ourselves! I will always have an attitude toward terrorist Richard Reed, who wore a shoe bomb on a flight. Now, we all have to take off our shoes before we go through the scanner. Mr. Reed should be sent to prison and have the other inmates throw shoes at him every day at noon.

As a statement of protest, people have gone to extreme measures to keep from being frisked. One young woman wore a bikini through the security line, eliminating any hiding places for small amounts of explosives or AK-47s. A former porn start began undressing at the Oklahoma City Airport before they finally stopped her.

However, the most ridiculous security check happened at GHW Bush Airport in Houston, Texas the day we decided to fly Jennie home. She'd been at M.D. Anderson for over two weeks. Although the doctors all agreed that Jennie should not travel on a commercial plane, they also agreed that an Angel Flight on Thursday would be risky as well. We decided to attempt the commercial flight with a determination that overruled the medical advice we had been given.

By this time, Jennie's Hail Mary attempt at treatment had failed. Her body could no longer contain the vast amount of water in her system. Her legs had been swelling up for several weeks. Not only were her legs enormous, but they were beginning to develop huge blisters which was another means of her body releasing the fluid. She could not walk without assistance. Jennie was ready to go home.

Bonnie booked a flight for the three of us. Because they could not stop us, the doctors ordered the nurses to wrap both of Jennie's legs as tightly as they could with a stock-room full of gauze, athletic bandages and whatever else they could find. It took them hours to wrap her legs for the journey. The airline's requirement was that Jennie had to be able to walk onto the plane under her own strength—with no help. I truly believe Jennie was able to make those steps onto the plane by God's help and sheer courage and determination.

We were rushing to get the gate on time when the Security Guard pulled Jennie aside for a personal pat-down. This was not one of Houston's prouder moments. Jennie was in a wheelchair and was very pale and weak from all that she had been through. She looked as sick as she was. Her well-wrapped legs were extended straight out because that was the only way she could be comfortable. She could not have run if the building was on fire! No one looked less like a terrorist threat than my daughter.

Bonnie and I realized that Jennie would have to be pushed through the line a different way, so we were not surprised that a guard came and whisked Jennie to the side. What happened next blew us both away! The guard called other guards over for a more thorough search of Jennie, including the unwrapping of her legs. We tried to explain to the guard that the legs could not be unwrapped for medical reasons. We even told them that we were taking our daughter home to die. We begged them to just let her through. For about thirty minutes, there was a discussion going on about whether or not Jennie's legs needed to be unwrapped. The argument went from ridiculous to down-right stupid! If you are going to profile a terrorist, you would not choose a weak, mummified cancer patient! Finally, the guard gave in. She would allow it this time.

Now came the biggest challenge we faced that day—those final steps onto the plane. Bonnie wheeled Jennie as close to the entrance of the plane as she could. Jennie stood up and let go of the wheelchair. In ways that resembled a baby's first steps, Jennie put one foot in front of the other and shuffled to our seats in the front of the plane. She plopped down in exhaustion and pride. She had made it! We were going home.

The flight was long, but uneventful. We landed in Tulsa on time. Now the task was to get Jennie into a wheelchair, out to a waiting car and settled in at home. Waiting at the curb with his door open and the seat laid back was our friend Bill Johnson. Bill's wife, Cathy was also there to greet us. Exhausted, we loaded our things and headed, finally, for home. I rode home with Larry and Rita Barnes. I talked their legs off!

Angels of Mercy

AT HOME, WHEN Jennie was moved into her bedroom from the recliner in her living room, she could no longer take care of herself. Jennie's clothing and bedding had to be changed twice a day. At first, Bonnie, Robb and I would help turn Jennie on her side for this process to take place. Because the "clean up" process forced us to lay her on the side where the cancer was located, she would scream with pain each time it happened. As much as it hurt, I still remember her saying, "Thank you!" to her two Angels of Mercy.

Sometimes, you do not get to see angels at work, but sometimes you can see them clearly. Two of our dear friends, Kim Baker and Cathie Johnson, volunteered to come over each day to handle the changing process. They are both dear friends and Registered Nurses. With the greatest of care, they would gently walk Jennie through the painful ordeal.

There came a point when it was difficult for Bonnie and me to listen to Jennie cry. Robb continued to help quite often, but Kim and Cathie finally said to Bonnie and me, "We can handle this! Why don't you step out of the room or go home until this is over?"

We knew Jennie was in the best of hands, so we began leaving the room when our Angels got there. Like clockwork, the doorbell would ring at the same time every night. Our "nursing team" would greet us and then go into Jennie's room and begin. Edwina Louthan, a dear friend and a physical therapist, would come occasionally to give Jennie a back rub.

Along with other friends, Jennie's Thursday night "small group" members would come and sit with us. Shelly Ingmire, Linn Kane, Kristine Kramer and Kim Allen would sit quietly throughout Jennie's last days. I remember when Jennie was in JPMC, Linn sat and held Jennie's hand while she talked to her about the fear of dying. The group had become a regular part of Jennie's Thursday night schedule.

After Jennie's death, Bonnie bought angels for each person who helped make Jennie's last days more bearable. Our car trunk was full when we pulled away from the store. I do not believe that Chicago Cutlery store had seen that much business in a long time.

As a constant reminder of Jennie's presence in our lives, Bonnie buys a new angel in Jennie's honor at Christmas time. An angel just seems like a natural symbol of Jennie's life.

The other day I walked through the hallway of the Pediatric Oncology floor at OU Medical Center. Tenth floor is not where Jennie worked when she started her nursing career, but I really needed to walk those hallways where she first made an impact. I stopped at the nursing station. I did not know what I was trying to do, but I asked a student nurse if she remembered Jennie. Being new to the hospital, she did not have a reason to know Jen. I left a note that said, "If you remember Jennifer Schuneman, would you mind calling her Dad?" I left my cell phone number.

When I got to the car, I realized I wanted to place a reminder of Jennie's presence even when people have forgotten her over time. I am now looking for a special angel image or statue to place at the nursing desk of the three hospitals and four departments where Jennie worked. I hope you stay well enough that you never need to be admitted to any of the hospitals where she worked—the OU Medical Center, St. Francis, or JPMC. If you do need their services, look for an angel at the nursing station. That will be from Jennie!

The Day Jennie Died

THE DOCTORS TOLD us that with liver cancer the patient begins to sleep more and more and then slips into a coma, dying a peaceful death. We took comfort in the fact that at least Jennie would feel no pain while she was dying. Unfortunately, the doctors were wrong! For the last five weeks, Jennie had been awake quite often. She was definitely suffering. There was nothing peaceful about those days at all. Thursday, June 17, 2010 was one of those *not so new normal days* we had come to expect. I had a doctor's appointment in Tulsa around noon. Because nothing had seemed to change in weeks, I felt okay with going out of town for a short time.

That morning, while I was gone, Bonnie began to notice some changes in Jennie's condition that concerned her enough that she asked Cathie Johnson to come over and give her opinion. They were both concerned, but agreed to keep an eye on Jennie since everything was being done to keep her comfortable.

I got home from Tulsa about 2 p.m. I went into Jennie's bedroom to sit with her for a little bit. I immediately noticed that her breathing pattern had changed drastically. She was taking rapid, shallow breaths that none of us had seen before. She seemed to be struggling to breathe. I called out to Bonnie, "Bon, how long has Jennie been breathing like this?" When Bonnie came into the room, she quickly answered, "That just started!" We had a hospice nurse named Ke'vin, so we called her. Robb ran across the street to get Baba. Saint Mary was waiting with us already.

Robb, Bonnie, Ke'vin, Saint Mary, Baba and I sat around Jennie's bed. Ke'vin was at the foot of the bed. I was sitting in a chair while holding Jennie's right hand. Bonnie and Robb were standing on each side of the head of Jennie's bed. Baba was sitting in a chair. Bonnie and Robb whispered to Jennie words of comfort and love. There was a sacred silence in the room.

There is something very holy about watching a person die when she knows the Lord. Something different and profound was happening.

Bonnie asked Ke'vin, "Is she dying?" "She might be," Ke'vin said.

Bonnie would ask, "How long do we have?" Ke'vin would answer, "We just don't know."

I kept noticing that Ke'vin was lifting the blanket off of Jennie's feet to check something. I finally realized he was watching the blood circulation leaving Jennie's legs. Her legs were turning a dark purple. As the circulation was cutting off, the purple began to move up from Jennie's feet to her ankles, then her legs.

I began to *feel* the difference. Jennie's hand began to close with her fists becoming tighter and tighter. I kept trying to pull them back to a normal position until I realized it was part of the process. Jennie was not totally unconscious at that time. This was no peaceful coma. The angels did not come to visit us. We could hear no heavenly choir or feel some comforting presence. It was nothing like we expected.

Then it happened! Right before she breathed her final breath, Jennie smiled one last time. She had her eyes open when it happened as if she was seeing something that we could not see. Bonnie called out, "Did you see that? Did you see her smile?" I was in a position where I could not see Jennie's face, but everyone else in the room agreed with Bonnie. My little angel faced death with a smile. It was 3:45 p.m. in the central time zone on earth when Jennie arrived in heaven.

Much like the first words Bonnie ever spoke to Jennie, Bonnie cried out, "You made it, Baby Girl! You made it! You made it, Baby Girl! You made it!" We openly wept as the reality of what had just happened sunk in.

We were paralyzed with grief.

Someone called Brown-Walker Funeral Home. They sent a hearse to pick up Jennie's body. The man that came was Melvin Nichols, a good friend of mine and the owner of Living Word, our local Christian bookstore. If it had to be done, I could not think of a better person to take care of the body.

As soon as the funeral home workers arrived, Bonnie led all of us out of the room and over to our house next door. Again, my wife is one of the strongest people that I have ever known. Even when her heart is breaking, she will take care of the business at hand. This moment was no different. When you take a Band-Aid off, it is going to hurt either way, but the least amount of pain comes from pulling it off quickly. Realizing that she could not bear to watch Jennie's body be removed, she had us step out of the house and let the funeral workers do what they had to do. We went home to cry and start making phone calls to notify the family.

I called my sister Judy. When I dialed my sister's number, I realized how busy she had to be preparing for her daughter Mendy's wedding, just two days away. I could not think of any way to soften the blow, so when Judy answered, I blubbered out, "Judy, Jennie just died!"

Not wanting to believe that what I had said was true, Judy responded, "Oh no, Randy, tell me it isn't so!"

Then, I made a very special request, "Judy, could they burn a candle in Jennie's memory at Mendy's wedding?" Quickly, Judy obliged. Regretfully, we were not able to attend the wedding, but a very special moment was given in Jennie's honor, explaining the significance of the candle. On the anniversary of Jennie's death, Mendy sent a beautiful note explaining how this week in June will always be a bittersweet one for her. The happiest moment of her life was getting married to Tomy. The saddest moment was in losing her sweet cousin Jennie. I will always cherish that card.

Have you ever seen an angel smile? We have! It will bring hope in the deepest hour of despair. We have often wondered, "What did Jennie see when she smiled?" Was it the angels that God had sent to get her? Was it Jesus Himself? Was it Gammy? Was it heaven? We will never know for sure until we get there, but knowing Jennie, she will give us a full report of every detail. Then, I am sure she will take us on the Grand Tour to introduce us to Jesus, reunite us with family and show us the heavenly corridors with a radiant smile on her face!

If we had our heart's desire, we would have asked for Jennie to just close her eyes and wake up in heaven. Instead, Jennie opened her eyes and drank in every detail of the journey.

Thank you, Lord for that angelic smile that was shared before she left us. Help us someday to see what she sees.

You made it, Baby Girl! You did make it!

Yes, her hair IS naturally curly!

Jennie at 3 in red dress with her legs crossed "My favorite picture of Jennie as a little girl. She is just a few weeks shy of her fourth birthday and the discovery of her cancer.

Jennie in pajamas with her baldhead and chicken pox marks.
The day after Jennie's fever broke from chicken pox.

Her smile made every day better!

Jennie and Jonah White. Look closely and you will see Jonah's water gun.

Jennie and her beloved Charlie at Christmas

Jennie with the rescued litter from the farm.

Jennie and Charlie at the lake.
This picture is on Jennie's grave marker.

Nurse Jennie in her favorite pink.

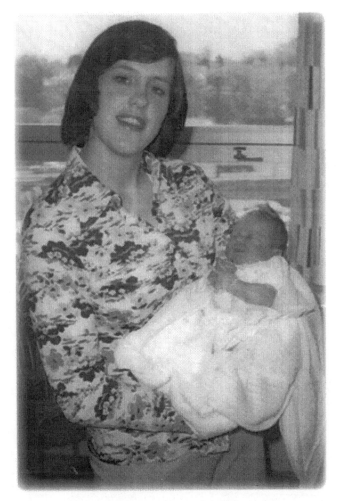

Bonnie with her Baby Girl

The Mischief Makers Club . . . do not let their size fool you.
Can you spell TROUBLE?

The Mischief Makers all grown up . . . sort of!

The Last Dance

The women in Korea all loved Jennie's eyes!

Part Two: Grief

God's Pre-Emptive Strike

The Sanctuary

A few come expecting entertainment, while others come to catch up on
their sleep. They say it's just a place you're supposed to go on Sundays.
Many are anxious to depart from this place and get home to
lunch, the television, and their Sunday afternoon naps.

But I am often reluctant to leave this place.
I see past the pews, the lights, the outward appearance.
Here I find peace and contentment for my soul.

Alone, I come when frustration, loneliness, depression,
and confusion have overwhelmed me.
Breaking the soothing silence, my fingers move over
the ivory keys of the magnificent piano.
With only God to listen,
I play better than I ever have before a human audience.

Putting all my energy and heart into the songs of praise, I leave
the world far behind me, for just a little while. Then, I stop.
As the wind blows outside, the building creaks, and then all is still.

The room is completely dark, except for the radiant light that
shines through the stained-glass windows. Closing my eyes,
I drink in His presence, and my troubled soul finds rest at last. "Amen."

A Deeper Kind of Grace

IT WAS JOHN Wesley who coined the phrase "prevenient grace." After decades of observing and journaling about his observations of how God worked in people's lives, Wesley concluded that God not only provided for our salvation on the Cross, but that His grace "went before" us, leading us to our salvation. The word "prevenient" comes from the root word "prevent." However, in Wesley's day, the meaning of the word was the opposite of today. Instead of meaning to stop something from happening, the word "prevent" focused on enabling something to happen.

Prevenient grace describes the wooing of God, and the preparation by God, to extend to all mankind the offer of a personal relationship with Him. Free will is man's God-given ability to choose how to respond to that invitation, either through acceptance or rejection.

After putting his observations through what pastors call the "REST test" (Reason, Experience, Scripture and Tradition), Wesley concluded that long before we responded to His love, God was sending people and circumstances into our lives to reveal His love for us. We can reject His leading, but God will give ample opportunities for us to respond to His offer.

Of all the theological truths that I would later study in preparation for ministry, I understood Prevenient Grace the most. Through my parents' example, I learned about faithfulness. Through Esther Yarbrough, I learned about unconditional love. Through the death of Bill Allen, I learned about mortality. God is working and wooing us throughout our life.

Throughout the last two years, I have sensed God preparing me for His next step in my life. In the next few chapters, I'll share some examples.

The Return of the Waltons

UNTIL THE HUXTABLES came along on *The Cosby Show*, the Waltons were my favorite television family. A three-generational family living and loving in the same big house, they were struggling together to survive the Great Depression and eventually World War II. If you were a fan of *The Waltons*, then you know that the show's most memorable *trademarks* were its opening and its closing.

At the beginning of each episode, Earl Hamner, the creator of the show, would introduce the story as the voice of "John Boy" Walton describing his family and the times in which they lived. At the end of each episode, they would show the big farm house at night. Just a few lights were on. Then you could hear the family telling each other "Good Night."

"Good Night, Mary Ellen!" "Good Night, John Boy!" "Good Night, Ben!"

"Good Night, John Boy!"

One by one, the lights would go out until all was dark. The theme song would begin to play and the credits would begin to roll. When all was finally quiet, any person with a heart would have wanted to be a part of that family. There was respect by the children to the parents, including John Walton to Grandpa Walton. The Walton family worked together in spite of the storms all around them. There were times when stress filled their lives, but the family always stayed together. They recognized the importance of family and enjoyed the privilege they had of being close.

The other trademark for me was the family sitting together at that large supper table for their meals. The women-folk prepared a large meal with all the fixin's. Although the food was delicious, being together was the most important thing. There were no soccer games to rush off to or television programs that vied for their attention. There were no cell phones or text messages or television or "social media." The Walton family's evenings were spent being together to eat and talk and *maybe* listen to the radio.

Oh, for the good old days!

Without us realizing how wonderful a gift it would be, the Schuneman family received a Walton Family season from God. First, Bonnie's Dad, Harold Mullins (a.k.a. Baba or Bobs) had decided he was near to selling the farm that he and Bernice (a.k.a. Bonnie's Mom or Gammy) had owned for 65 years. After the death of his wife, Baba felt it was time to move on to the next phase of his life. His first step was to purchase a home he could move to after the farm sold. Much to our surprise and pleasure, Baba bought the house across the street from us. Our good friends and neighbors, Rita and Larry Barnes, had decided to move to another subdivision nearby. They gave Baba first choice on purchasing the home, and he took it!

For Baba, everything has to have a name. He had a sheep named Sheepy, a horse named Colty and the house at 5308 Richmond Drive could be no different. Baba christened it "Me-shack." For about a year, Baba would spend an occasional weekend at his *city* home and the rest of the time at the ranch. Finally, an offer was made and accepted for the farm. The land sold. All the remaining cattle sold the day before the machinery auction. Bob was able to mount Colty and drive the last head of cattle into the corral. The transition was like a whirlwind!

The auction was held on June 1, 2009 and included the sale of everything that was not nailed down (and some things that were). A tractor, hay hauler, disc, plow, combine and tons of odds and ends sold in a matter of a few hours. Like a hurricane hitting the Eastern Coast, the family loaded up the remaining items that were going with Baba and headed for Bartlesville and the newly-formed Schuneman Compound.

Jennie had already moved to Bartlesville and had bought a 1939 home that was close to the High School. We enjoyed having Jennie ten minutes away, but when our next-door neighbor Nancy informed us that she was retiring and moving to Minnesota, Bonnie began to ponder how great it would be to have Jennie as our neighbor as well. We made a verbal agreement to buy the house when Nancy was ready to move. We even settled on a price.

We tried to sell Jennie's house "By Owner," but the one serious showing was cancelled because the real estate agent fell ill. Then, when we chose to use a realty company, the house sold in two hours—to the same people who had missed the previous meeting! When the dust settled, Jennie moved in as our next-door neighbor, a month after Baba settled in Me-Shack. Now

I could open *three* garage doors from the convenience of my car! It was a joy to spend time with Jennie each evening and hear about her day.

Then Robb came home shortly after Jennie moved into her new house. Robb had been in South Korea for three years teaching English as a Second Language. He had taught children and teens at first, but spent the last year and a half teaching adults. No matter what the age group, though, everybody loves Robbie. He has a natural gift with children, coolness around teens and an ability to communicate well with adults. Bonnie, Jennie and I had traveled to South Korea in 2008. It made me even prouder of my son when I realized the food he had come to enjoy. On our trip, hearing the words "traditional Korean meal" struck fear in our hearts and stomachs.

So before long, we settled into a predictable routine. We would wait for Jennie to come home. She would be wearing her blue scrubs and the bonnet which I always teased her about. When Jennie took the cap off, she looked like she was still running. It stuck straight out instead of relaxing. Our family would greet her with our usual, "Welcome home, JD!"

Like the Waltons, Jennie would answer, "Hello, Daddy! Hello, Momma! Hello, Robbie!" and "Hello, Bubba!" You could feel energy coming into the room. Somehow everything seemed a little better for all of us when Jennie got home.

Bonnie was not going to let her Dad get *skinny* on *her* watch, so each evening included a gorgeous meal, including dessert. We would sit around the table and talk about our day. That's when Jennie usually covered every detail of her day, a routine that I've enjoyed and recounted in these pages. The memory is precious.

Then, depending on what time Jennie got home, we would all watch *Wheel of Fortune*, either live or recorded. On an adventurous night, we would watch two episodes of *Wheel* back-to-back. This might sound boring, but watching *Wheel* with Jennie was a fun experience. She was a fantastic puzzle-solver! Our family divided up into teams, but whoever was Jennie's teammate would inevitably win. If she knew the puzzle, she would shout it out rapid-fire like a machine gun, so there could be no question of her victory.

Jennie also had some responses to certain categories of *Wheel*. When it was a Prize Puzzle, she would shout out, "Prize puzzle? I love prize puzzles." When the "Before and After" category came into play, she would say, "Before and After? That's my favorite." This gentle-spirited, shy young lady would become as fearsome as a pit bull. She would rejoice with each victory she had, but in a non-offensive way. Or, rather, sometimes it actually *was* offensive when she won every round. Sometimes, *Wheel* would take us up all the way to 7 p.m.!

No evening would be complete without some table games. We usually played Sabotage or Rook or Mexican Train, a game with dominoes. Because of the nature of the games, it was not a given as to who the winner would be. In fact, Jennie was a rookie Rook player. We could take advantage of her lack of skills in the game until she started understanding the strategies that could be used. Then, she held her own.

Most nights, we also played *First Star*. Sitting out on the back porch, we would compete with each other on who spotted the first star each night. Clouds factor in, so that it is not always the same star that appears first. It is harder than you think.

The party usually broke up around 9 p.m. so Baba could walk across the street to go to bed. After a few months, we realized that Jennie was going to sleep on our couch before she went home. We just thought she was exhausted from the day. Looking back, it probably was an early sign of things to come.

Life was as perfect as it could be for us. Our kids were safe. We could see them every day without getting in the car. They were attending church with us. Baba seemed to be adjusting well to his new surroundings. Family would drop by from time to time. Bonnie's first cousin, Mary Mullins, whom we called Saint Mary, had moved to Bartlesville and would join us on several occasions. We especially loved it when the Saint would bring food or a dessert for us to enjoy.

For about nine of the last eleven months of Jennie's life, we were living the *Waltons* life. It was during this time that I myself became quite ill. I had suffered a related disease in 1996. In that year, I contracted the EN syndrome. Some call it the Empty Nest, but it sounds worse if I just use the initials. I first felt the onset of EN when we took Jennie to Spring Arbor College (now University). It was hard enough saying goodbye, but SAU has a traditional Oak Tree Ceremony where the freshman students are called up in small groups and led away to get to know their fellow students. What Bonnie and I did not realize is that when your child's name is called, they *kidnap* your child. Your baby girl is *ripped* from your arms and sent to a *concentration camp*. You are not supposed to make contact with them in any way *for six weeks*.

The ceremony was on a Saturday. I did the best I could, but I met Jennie at McDonald's on Tuesday of the next week.

With Robbie, I suffered severe EN when he left to go to South Korea. For the first time, I could not get in my car and at least drive to meet him. Olivet Nazarene University was five hours away, but at least I could see him if I wanted to make the drive. Robb had learned about the teaching job at the beginning of June 2005 and reported for duty the last week of June. So many details had to be taken care of before he left. As only Robb can do, everything happened just in time. His passport was the last item. He picked it up at the post office at 5:30 p.m. even though the post office closed at 5, just in time to head for his departure.

Our immediate family had gone out to eat the night before he flew out. In the middle of our normal conversation, Robb stopped in mid-sentence and said, "What the heck! I am going to South Korea." If I could have, I would have restrained him from going, but once he was safely there I didn't worry about him as much. He has a knack for taking care of himself.

Before anyone started moving in, Bonnie and I had adjusted to the EN syndrome pretty well. We could eat a four-cheese Tony's pizza with a little hamburger added for supper. We only had two schedules to keep. Both kids were taking care of themselves financially. It was just *me and the little lady*. We could go around singing, "Just the Two of Us" with great gusto. If I needed to, I could take a road trip to Spring Arbor and be back before night fall.

When everyone was moved in, I was stricken with another devastating disease. I came down with a bad case of *FOTL syndrome*. While every parent experiences the Empty Nest syndrome, not all parents struggle with FOTL. In fact it affects men far more than women. Its symptoms include shortness of breath and a need to be alone. A friend who was going through far more complicated circumstances than me described it best when he said, "I just want to be able to walk around my own house in my underwear!" *Fruit of the Loom syndrome* is usually like the flu—it's over in a short time. Once the adjustment to the new structure was made, everything was fine.

Looking back, I can see clearly how God gave our family a special gift of time together. I cherish those days before Jennie became ill as sacred. We take so many daily gifts for granted: a hug, a laugh, a new day. My Dad always reminded me, "There is no better feeling than having your children safe under your roof." He is right! If I had those days to live over, I would hug a little longer, laugh a little louder and say, "I love you!" a million times a day. As it is, I think about those evenings and have to smile at what God gave us.

I do not know if we ever sleep in heaven, but if we do, I look forward to hearing, "Good night, Daddy!"

"Good Night, Jen!" "Good night, Momma!" "Good night, Jenjen!" "Good night, Bubba!" "Good night, Hehe!"

Angelic Visitations

IN THE FALL of 2006, my mother-in-law, Bernice Mullins (or Gammy, as we called her), was taken to the hospital in Stillwater, Oklahoma with a severe leg problem. Over the next few weeks, her health began to decline quickly. The spot on her leg began to cave in. Over the previous years, her spine had degenerated to the point that she had to use an electric wheelchair around the house. Her eyes were also degenerating, making it hard for her to read her Bible. Every time she came against a physical challenge, she was able to find ways to overcome and adjust to the new set of events.

However, this time things seemed different. The doctors struggled to find a method by which they could stop the hole in Gammy's leg from enlarging. It took months to find a solution that would restore her leg to health enough that she could go home from the hospital. Not only was the severity of the physical problem great, but Gams seemed to be losing her will to live. Certainly no one would have blamed her for giving up. She had lost her ability to walk. Her eyesight made it almost impossible to read. Her hands shook from a hereditary disease that made it difficult for her to feed herself. It was embarrassing for Gams to eat in public.

I truly believe the family, especially her daughters, talked Gammy into regaining her will to live. My mother-in-law was one of the emotionally strongest women I have been privileged to know. Bonnie inherited that trait from her Mom. Gammy's Father was an oil executive for Conoco Petroleum Company. Because of his position, the Isaacs family never felt the impact of the Great Depression. Her family had a maid. They were very cultured. In fact, they had a family orchestra that traveled the surrounding area. They were exceptionally talented.

Then Gammy fell in love with a farmer. He was a handsome farmer, but a farmer nonetheless. Farmers tend to live on farms. When Gams fell in love with Baba, she moved with him to a small acreage about 17 miles from civilization. Gammy transitioned from pearls to plows. There were many difficult years when the family tried to survive. Gams endured through crop failures, floods, tornadoes, a miscarriage and the daily toil of all life on the farm. Three big meals a day being carried to the field for the harvest were just part of that routine. Because, as Bonnie puts it, Gammy was *farm stock*—a woman who had withstood so many tough times—she was a survivor! But now the challenge seemed too great.

It was during that long stay in the Stillwater hospital that Gammy had a visit from an angel. Because she had been so sick, the family thought it might have been a hallucination from the medicine. However, for the next year, Gammy would talk about her angel. She could give a full description: red, flowing hair, flowing robe and . . . wings! No one could take from her the reality that she had been visited by an angel.

Somewhere during that year, Bonnie was flipping through a magazine with Gammy. At one point, Gams told Bonnie to go back to a previous page. Gammy pointed and exclaimed, "That is my angel! That is exactly what she looks like!" Bonnie tore out the picture and kept it in a safe place. The family became more convinced that Gammy's Angel was real.

I truly believe that Gammy willed herself through the next year. She wanted to experience one more Thanksgiving, one more Birthday, one more Wedding Anniversary and especially one more Christmas. Her leg improved miraculously. She drank in every time the family was together. We took some friends down to the farm for a short visit. Gammy did not say much until a door opened in the conversation to talk about family memories. Her eyes lit up and she began to tell story after story.

It caught the whole family off-guard when Gams was taken to the Stillwater Hospital in early November 2007. Her symptoms were flu-like. I think all of us thought it would be a short stay and then we would return to our routine. She was admitted into the hospital on Wednesday. On Thursday morning, things seemed to be going well enough that Baba went back to the farm to work. Bonnie's breath was taken away when the doctor came into the room to talk about end-of-life issues. Gammy was dying? She only has days to live? What?

The rest of us were called in immediately. That night, Baba and Gammy had their talk. Gammy asked, "Do you think this could be it?"

Baba answered, "It could be."

Then the two soul mates, who had shared over sixty years of marriage, had time to talk about how deeply they loved each other. They both would

147

have done it all over again. It was one of those moments when you talk from the heart and hold nothing back. There may not be any more time.

On that Thursday night, Bonnie stayed in the hospital room with Bernice. During the night, Bernice said, "My angel is here!"

Bonnie said, "Where is she, Mom?" "She's at the foot of my bed."

"Can I see her?" Bonnie asked.

Settling back, Gams said, "No. She's gone now."

On Friday, November 2, 2007, Gammy visited with the family in the morning. She slipped into a semi-coma in the early afternoon, still conscious of the conversation as she reacted with her eyes. That evening, with her husband holding her head in his hands and the family gathered round, Jennie Bernice Mullins rested in the hands of Jesus.

A few days later, "Saint" Mary Mullins, Bonnie's double cousin, went to visit her Mother. Genevieve Mullins was Gammy's sister. Although Bernice and Genevieve had been neighbors for many years, Genevieve was in a nursing home suffering from Alzheimer's. Mary never told her mom that Bernice had passed away. Genevieve never knew about the funeral. However, on this visit, Genevieve asked, "How is Bernice doing?"

Knowing her mother did not need anything to upset her, Mary answered, "Bernice is doing fine!"

Genevieve responded, "I thought so. We have had such good visits these last few days."

Mary asked, "You saw Bernice?"

Genevieve added, "Yes, she came to visit me here."

I do not know if you believe in angels or not, but I do now! At Bernice's funeral, they distributed bookmarks of *Gammy's Angel*. We found comfort in the thought that God sent an angel to comfort and accompany Gammy on her journey home.

As I have mentioned earlier, God spoke to me through two dreams when Jennie was first diagnosed with ovarian cancer. When Jennie was four, I had this calm assurance that no matter what, she would survive the cancer and the treatment. It was a joyful experience to tell others how God gave me an assurance throughout those two years.

But God did not speak this time! No word of encouragement or hope was given. After Jennie died, I longed for a sign from God that Jennie was all right. I wanted to dream about her or have her visit our bedroom—something—anything! But nothing happened.

On Tuesday, June 22, 2010, we had a graveside service for Jennie before the celebration service on Wednesday. After the drive to Ponca

City, family and friends were invited back to Bartlesville for a full dinner. During that meal time, our great niece Rachel approached me and pulled on my hand. I leaned down to talk to Rachel when she said, "Uncle Randy, I need to tell you something, but we must go to a Secret Place." We did not have a specified Secret Place, so Rachel and I went over to a corner of the room.

Rachel said, "You cannot tell anybody this, but I had a dream last night. I saw Jennie and Gammy walking together. They were happy!" Oh, I needed to hear that! I hugged Rachel and cherished her words in my heart.

Our former neighbor and good friend, Rita Thurman Barnes, told me she had dreams all week about Jennie. Jennie was working in a garden and was enjoying herself to the hilt. That helped so much. I think she was planting sunflower seeds.

However, I wanted a visitation of my own! God did not answer that request immediately, but a few weeks after Jennie's death, I did have a dream in which I got a glimpse of Jennie. It was one of those where you know who the person is, even if you can't see her well. A few months later, my dream was about Jennie walking down the hall explaining her condition to some friends. She talked about what procedures they were going to do. Like a doctor on rounds, Jennie was very calm about everything.

God even used Facebook to visit with me. One day, I was doing my routine web surfing when I saw a little section at the top right side of the screen. It was entitled, *Important Comments from Friends.* I recognized some comments I had read before. I saw a comment I do not remember ever seeing. It was from Jennie's Facebook page. It read, "I am enjoying my brand new home." I had never seen that section before and have not seen it since. You will never know how I needed that message that day.

A few days before Jennie's 33rd birthday, I was experiencing nightmares for three nights in a row. The dreams were about leaving the pastorate and other events. The day before Jennie's birthday, I had a dream in which I saw Jennie dancing. It was in silhouette, but I could see her twirling and moving gracefully before me. I woke up with a smile and the nightmares stopped!

My Mom and Dad joined Robbie and me on Memorial Day to visit Jennie's grave. That day was far more emotional than I had ever thought it would be. That night, I had a dream about Jennie. She was healthy and just waking up from a good nap. I walked over to her and lifted up her head while giving her a kiss on the forehead. The neat thing about that dream is that I could feel her hair. Also, I could feel the kiss against her skin!

While I was driving one day, I noticed that the car ahead of me had a license plate that read, "RN JEN." I took pictures with my cell phone so I could be reminded of Jennie's JENRN license plate. The similarity made me smile.

We received a letter meant for Jennie about seven days after her death. It was an insurance company letter letting her know that they hoped to "re-connect" with her as a customer. It clearly displayed Jennie's name and address. The phrase on the outside of the envelope read, "We want you back!" I do too!

I called Jennie's old cell number just out of curiosity with hope that I might hear a left-over voice mail. Of course, I got a message saying "this number is not available or out of service." I had no way to respond to that information. Later that day, I got a voice mail from a man who had Jennie's old number. The man said, "Randy, I don't know you, but you got a wrong number." How did he know my name was Randy? My call log shows that I got a call from Jennie Schuneman eight months after she died. That information will never be erased from my phone.

I know it will not happen on a regular basis, but when God gives me an *angelic visitation,* I want to enjoy every moment of it. That's as good as it gets on this side of heaven!

I Just Can't Do This!

SHORTLY AFTER JENNIE signed the necessary documents to transfer her earthly possessions to Bonnie and me, things began to change drastically. All of the sudden, my very articulate daughter could not finish a sentence! She would say, "I believe that . . ." or "I think . . ." She never completely lost her ability to communicate until the very end, but Jennie would only speak randomly.

When my parents came to visit, Jennie recognized them and said, "Hi, Meemaw! Hi, Poppy!" My sister-in-law stayed with Jennie one afternoon. Jenarold, whom we call Nana, spent her time with Jennie singing to her. When Nan was finished, Jennie said, "That was pretty, Nana!" And Jennie seemed to recognize children when they came to visit.

But there was no denying that Jennie's condition was declining. She dozed off and on. When she was awake, she struggled to try to communicate the smallest thought through hand motions. There was a noticeable loss of weight. She was able to keep ice chips down some of the time, but she couldn't eat. She looked like a person who was dying! Her hair was coming out again from the one chemotherapy treatment. She was gaunt and pale. She had that "look" around her eyes that people get before they die.

There came a point when it was impossible for me to stay in the room with Jennie. I prayed that she would be asleep when I stepped in, because it tore me apart to see her suffering. It was during this time that Robbie stepped in to a circumstance that I was unable to handle. I watched Robb exhibit a strength that was far beyond what I could muster. He stayed with Jennie nearly 24-7. He slept in her room with her! He slept in a chair most of the time. He would lean near to her ear and say, "Jennie, it is all right. You are here in your beautiful home! We are here for you."

Although her heart was breaking, Bonnie stood beside Jennie's bedside constantly. Jennie would be able to keep down the water from the ice chips quite often, but she also would vomit up the water at times. Bonnie and Robbie faithfully stood by Jennie and comforted her. I know Jennie was scared. I wanted to be there for her, but I would walk in and out of the room nervously to try to avoid facing the situation. It hurt too deeply.

I have always known in my heart that Robbie was an amazing person. While I like to "play it safe," Robb loves adventure. Robb and I got lost in downtown Tulsa once while we were walking. I became frantic! Robb calmly said, "Dad, don't worry. Just look at this as an adventure!" While I was arguing about how desperate our situation was, Robb pointed to our car and said, "There it is, Dad. Now wasn't that fun?"

I knew Robb had this incredible knack to land on his feet. Whether he was in South Korea or Portland, Oregon, he figured out how to make it to where he was headed. While I was trying to protect him, he was making his way just fine. He did not have the problem . . . I did.

Okay, I do have the problem. But in those difficult days of Jennie's suffering, Robb showed the depth of his character by remaining Jennie's constant cheerleader and comforter. When I could not, Robb did!

Something happened to my son that started when he left home for college. It accelerated when he went to South Korea for three years. It deepened when his sister needed him to really be her brother. He grew up! He changed from a boy to a man. I realize that I truly struggled with that fact. Jennie always stayed 12 around me. Robb had already become a man, in spite of my best efforts to keep it from happening.

I do not know how I would have survived those horrible days had it not been for my son. Thank you Robb for being the man I just could not be at the time! Chow Ching!

The Firsts

A Perfect Creation

Father--such a common word that too many times we tend to take for
granted these wonderful people, our comforters, teachers, and friends.
Long ago, God had a plan,
'cause from the start He knew that though He was our
heavenly Father, we needed earthly ones, too.
He gave them two eyes to watch over us with protective love and care.
Two ears to listen whenever we had a burden we needed to share.
Voices to read us bedtime stories
'til we finally ceased to squirm.
And sometimes when we were naughty, those gentle voices became firm.
Whiskers on a stubbly chin that always seemed to tickle.
A mouth packed full of endless jokes that always made us giggle.
Two legs to chase us through the yard while getting some exercise.
A lap for us to sit on that seemed to be just the right size.
Two arms that were always ready to enfold us when we needed them so.
Two hands that knew when to hold onto us and when to let us go.
Then God mixed all the various parts which I have
mentioned above, and tied them together with a generous
heart overflowing with unconditional love.
At last, a human figure stood, when God's work was finally done.
He named the figure "Father" and gave this perfect creation to everyone.
So remember yours this Father's Day. Before the day
is through, tell him just how special he is.
After all, he's a gift from God to you.

The First Time Ever I Saw . . .

ROBERTA FLACK RECORDED a song a few years back entitled "The First Time Ever I Saw Your Face." I thought it was a love song, but after listening to it several times I realized that it was written for biology class. After talking about the man's face, she began focusing on other parts of his anatomy. Anyway, the song deals with the emotions that come with experiencing something—in this case love—for the first time. Obviously for Ms. Flack, this experience was very positive.

Not all "first times" are enjoyable. Most first dates are awkward. The first day at a new school can be very lonely. The first dentist appointment can even be painful. The reality is that life is full of "first times." But if we did not have first dates, we would never have fallen in love with our spouse. If we did not experience that first day at school, we never have made those lifetime friends we know as "school buddies." If we never saw the dentist for the first time, we would never know how wonderful it is to experience the relief from pain.

In order to understand the grieving process, a person needs to prepare themselves for the mile markers known as "the firsts." The first time a person experiences special days or places after losing a loved one can be very difficult. Knowing that these days are coming does not eliminate all the pain, but at least it can give us a "heads up" to better prepare for those days.

We had celebrated Jennie's thirty-second birthday two months before she died. We were several months away from Thanksgiving, Christmas or other major holidays, but we were faced with the most unusual Fourth of July I ever hope to experience. It was excruciating for me and my family to "restart our engines" so soon after Jennie's death. Here is an overview of our "firsts."

155

I've Fallen and I Can't Get Up!

The first Fourth of July and back to the pulpit

ON SUNDAY, JULY 4, 2010, I woke up drenched in sweat. As hard as I tried, I could not make myself get out of bed. I was paralyzed with fear! I found it hard to breathe and even harder to think about putting a suit on and heading to the church. It was not going to be a *hard* day. Because of the holiday, there was no Sunday School, no evening service, no committee meetings and just *one sermon*. That is what had me pinned . . . the sermon! It had been seventeen days since Jennie had died, but three months since I had been in the pulpit. The Church Board had been very kind to let me have all the time off I needed during Jennie's ill- ness. However, it seemed a natural re-start date since the Fourth of July is always a slow Sunday. Lots of people are out of town or out at the lake.

Normally, preaching comes natural to me. When I was called to preach at sixteen, I had been anxiously waiting for that confirmation since I was five. The year before I started first grade, Esther Yarbrough, our pastor's wife, watched me while Mom was teaching school. Mrs. Y. would let me stay in the sanctuary while she cleaned the church. Every day, I would pull a chair up behind the pulpit and "hold services." I led singing, took offering and preached Monday through Friday. Our family even made the front page of the *Medford Patriot Star* with our picture included. The caption said " . . . and Randy wants to be a preacher." I was seven.

What had me beside myself that morning was the thought of being totally vulnerable for 25 to 30 minutes. What if I cry? What if I lose my train of thought? What if I cannot make sense? For me, it was just seventeen days to process what had happened to our family in the last three months. For most in the congregation, it was good to have the pastor back after three months. That is understandable. Everybody likes *normal*, including me. The only problem is that for those who have lost a loved one, things will never be the same again! The common phrase seems to be, "We want our old pastor back!" Why aren't you smiling like you used to? Why did you not give me your full attention when I was telling you about my Aunt Josephine's hangnail? Why did you rush off to your office instead of shaking hands with the people? The truth is that the *old pastor* will not be back. Death changes everything! So many things that are the *measuring stick* of success for a pastor do not matter anymore. When we thought that Jennie was going to die shortly after Easter, how many attended Easter Sunday service held no significance. The financial condition of the church was nowhere on my radar. Being a *vision-caster* for the congregation was not on my Top Ten List of priorities. Very few things mattered!

I am sure there are other professions where this is true, but for a pastor, there is a certain *game face* that is expected. No one wants to be pulled over for speeding by a police officer who just had a fight with his wife! We expect our policeman to stay calm no matter what we do or say to them. If they react, a policeman will usually end up on the evening news. Can you imagine a surgeon concluding his pre-op remarks by saying, "I hope this goes well. It's the first time I have ever tried a procedure like this." Nervous surgeons make us nervous, right? We want our surgeon to be stoic and extremely confident in their ability (with just a little white hair to show experience).

Most people have their pre-conceived notion of how a pastor should look and act. Pastors are not to be *angry*. Like a policeman, they are to stay calm no matter what has been said or done to them. Plus, they are to *smile* no matter how tough the day, while saying, "God bless you, my brother." Pastors are to be *perfect parents* even though they seldom get to sit with their spouse or children during service. Although my children have been treated well throughout my pastoral career, many churches seem to select a committee to watch and report on the *Preacher's Kids*. Pastors are held to a higher standard than anyone else in the church.

One of the expectations is that pastors are not supposed to be *wounded*. When we go to the hospital, we are to stand beside the bed, not be in it. Being wounded is not in the job description. I heard of one Church Board that gave their Pastor two weeks to "get over it" when his son was shot and killed. I used to tell people, "I was human before I began pastoring." Some people took that to mean that I thought I was superhuman! My point was that I am still human. Being a pastor does not make anyone immune from emotions. Pastors do not handle the death of a family member any different than any other member of the congregation. We just examine them more carefully.

I had an associate pastor who found out that his son had been killed in a plane crash while watching the local evening news. Before the family was contacted, the news station played an audio recording of his son's last words before the crash. What a heart-wrenching tragedy! The associate pastor tried to take the *ministerial approach* to suffering. He acted like he thought people would expect him to. He showed no emotions. He never showed a sign of pain or weakness. He would say things like, "This must be God's Will!" His unwillingness to express his emotions began to destroy his health. He would not allow himself to suffer, because he thought people would question his walk with Christ.

Isn't it the pastor's responsibility to share with us about God's blessings and make us feel better? Especially today when it is popular to question the essentials of the faith, pastors should stay away from controversial topics like Hell or Suffering. Most importantly, whatever the pastor is go- ing to do should be able to be done before noon! Holding service until 12:15 p.m. will get you chastised. Everyone knows that the Dallas Cowboys kick-off at noon, right?

So what do you do as a broken-hearted pastor when it is Sunday and you have to preach? You get up, get dressed, put your best smile on your face and try to act as if everything in your life is back to normal. Since retiring, I have had friends tell me they wanted to stop the service, because they were hurting so badly for me. As I sat through the beginning of the service, I tried to keep from crying, because I knew if I got started it would be hard to stop.

When it was the time for the sermon, I put my best effort into trying to hide from the congregation what was going on in my heart. I believe my heart was as well-hidden as the toupee that Brother Johnson wears on Sunday. You know, the one where no human being has ever had that much hair, including Absalom. As I stood alone to preach, I was bleeding from chambers of my heart that I did not know existed. It was a very painful experience for many in the congregation as they watched me struggle and could not help me. Preaching would be difficult for the next three months. Even though some people said it was the best they had heard me preach, I was petrified every week. My goal was to teach my Sunday School class, *survive* the sermon and dash home.

Everything was tough especially during those first three months. Nine days after my first sermon, it was time for July's Church Board meeting.

There was only a brief time while I was at West Flint Church of the Nazarene that I ever *enjoyed* one of these meetings. This Board Meeting was more complicated than most. I had not attended one in three months. I didn't have enough strength to work through any major issues. Then, I had a panic attack. I knew I couldn't cancel it after missing three sessions. About mid-afternoon on that *second Tuesday of every month*, I struggled to get an agenda to Karen Dimond, the church secretary. Our meetings always started at 7 p.m. As late as 6:59 p.m. that night, I was honestly ready to bale. Maybe they would fail to notice I did not show!

Finally, I mustered the courage to get my notebook and head towards the classroom where the Board meets. I walked into the room and relaxed a little bit. Most of the people in the room were my friends; surely I could make it through a two hour meeting, right? I stuttered and stammered through most of the meeting. I do not think we got anything settled that night, but we did have a closing prayer and dismissed the meeting. Carson West, a friend who served on the Board, talked to me afterward. He said, "You seemed a little nervous tonight." He had no idea what an understatement that was!

The congregation was very patient about coming to me for counseling. They were willing to "talk to me later." Their patience was probably good for both of us. I was in no condition to give solid counsel. Also, it would have been hard for me to listen to their problems. I found myself sitting at my computer crying through a lot of days. I found some solace in writing *notes* to Jennie. Mostly it was just rambling something about how I was feeling, but it made the day a little more bearable.

Within the first six months after Jennie's death, I had several staff positions to replace with new personnel. God bless their hearts; they walked into the middle of my darkest hour. I have never been the epitome of organization, but I never did get a handle on helping the new staff members get settled in. The problem is that nothing really mattered! So much of pastoral ministry is driven by numerical statistics. How many? How much? These are the two questions that tend to measure success in ministry. I still loved the people, but I had no energy to *chase* them to get them into service.

The one thing I did not realize at the time was that the church was grieving as well. Along with suffering Jennie's death, they had lost Darren Melton, who had been the Music Associate for twelve years. A few months after I got back, Jade Rogers, the Youth Pastor, left to take a church. While I was trying to act as if everything was back to normal, I needed to recognize that we all were hurting. We did not need normal. We needed to learn how to suffer together.

The worst struggle was trying to fix the church. Finances were holding steady, but attendance had dropped. I exhausted myself trying to find a magic bullet that would get us back on track. I finally realized that I was not called to *fix the church*. That was God's doing!

I realize that grief comes in different ways for different people, but the first three months were horrible for me. I had questions about staying in pastoral ministry. I could not even think about the eight years until I retired—eight days seemed unbearable enough. My pastor friends all told me, "Don't make any major decisions in the first six months." Some days, their advice was all that I clung to.

Letting the Cat Out of the Bag

The first Thanksgiving

WHEN WE THINK of Thanksgiving, many images come to mind: NFL football, family, pumpkin pie and turkey with all the fixings. However, during Thanksgiving 2010, we had to deal with a cat, of all things. Not just any cat, but the one you try to keep "In The Bag" so no one will know about it. During the weeks leading up to Thanksgiving, Bonnie and I decided to buy a new home and were preparing to leave pastoral ministry. The home was finalized—to make it even more challenging, though, I hadn't even seen it before making the purchase. The cat—or better yet THE CAT—was bigger than any ordinary elephant in the room. No one at the church could know. Our "escape" needed to be "hush-hush" until we had time to think of a way to tell everybody.

One of things I was not prepared to do immediately was to tell my parents. "Mom and Dad, I am resigning from the church, retiring from pastoral ministry, plus we bought a house in Edmond, do not know how long it will take to sell our current house and do not have a job lined up, so we will have no income and no insurance for a little while." That's not exactly the perfect way to welcome in the Thanksgiving holiday.

My parents came to our house so that we could drive together to Branson, Missouri. Since my parents and Bonnie's parents had been friends for years, I took Mom and Dad over to say hello to Baba, my father-in-law, who had moved in across the street. Baba got coffee while my parents took a seat in the living room. Baba sat down and said, "Well, Don, I lived on the farm for 65 years and I could only make it in this house two years!" One word—*Awkward*!

My Mom turned to me and said, "Are you moving, too?" I have never been able to lie to my Mom. Well, not very well anyway. When I was twelve, I tried to hide the fact that I'd been wasting money on baseball cards, and I thought I'd gotten away with it with a small untruth. But when I was sixteen, I was sitting at the kitchen table with Mom when I blurted out, "You remember that day I said I had two packs of cards? I had ten—I'm sorry!" Mom had known all along, but she put her arms around me as I blubbered my confession.

Hiding a few packs of cards was one thing. Hiding a house is completely different! I answered, "Yes, Mom, we bought a house in Edmond. I am going to resign the pastorate here and move sometime in the future." Once again—*Awkward*! Fortunately for me, Mom went into shock and could not speak! But now we had a couple of days together in the car and then at Branson to work through this.

My sister, Judy Meisner, and her husband, Wes, joined us at a lovely house they had secured for us. We had a fun couple of days planned together, playing table games and enjoying the famous city. With Bonnie, my parents, and me knowing the news, it became a matter of when we were going to release the proverbial cat again. How do you properly tell your sister and her family that you are going to "have a few changes in your life?" Well, we just did it. Instead of waiting for the "perfect time," we just all dropped the "bomb" together.

"Sis," I said, "we are leaving pastoral ministry, bought a house in Edmond and will have no job!" I think I noticed that everyone in the room, except maybe Bonnie, took an immediate step away from me. It might have been a coincidence, but the response made me feel like I had just broken out with leprosy. I thought I heard someone start to call out, "Unclean! Unclean!" If I had the assurance then that I have now that God was in charge, I would have handled it differently. The decision was too fresh and too radical to feel very comfortable.

We enjoyed meals and table games throughout the couple of days. The topic kept coming up about the move. Maybe it was to make sure everyone had heard correctly. I was feeling good about the decision, but my head was spinning about what we would be facing. Everything in my life was about to change! The occupation that I had felt called to since I was 16, the desire to be a pastor which I had since I was 5, the city I lived in, the friends I had, the stories that were being written, it would all be totally different for me.

I knew that we were supposed to buy the house. I knew moving closer to family on both sides would be a good first step toward finding healing. I even knew that I could not heal under the circumstances I was experiencing. So many things that I could not control were changing around me. Worst of all, I was not sure I could not stay in the pastorate beyond February. That time frame seemed like an eternity.

Still, there was a sense of uncertainty that kept me from enjoying this Thanksgiving like I wished I could. Missing Jennie at this family event for the first time was difficult in and of itself, but missing her and having a complete "life make-over," made things even more difficult to face.

I was glad that Bonnie had an assurance about the house and the move. She was excited about having her "dream house" so early in our lives. Although I had never seen the house and property, I could tell that Bonnie had not been this happy since before Jennie died. I rested in the assurance that she was so sure about the decision and the timing. Her faith would help me feel more "anchored" in the decisions we had made. Now I just had to keep the cat "bagged" at Church!

The First Noel

The first Christmas

CHRISTMAS: DECORATED TREES, gifts, wonderful meals . . . family. Christmas is Jennie's favorite time of the year. She could be found searching for that perfect gift for each person throughout the entire year. I became "addicted" to Sudoku one year. I had worked through various First Level Sudoku puzzles and along with the "cheat sheets" in the back of the books, I had at least gotten the hang of the game. I just had one problem: I couldn't keep track of the books. I would lose them in the house. Jennie's solution? An electronic version of Sudoku. It even had a built-in "cheat" mechanism. What a perfect Christmas gift!

Most of the time, Robbie likes clothes or even bigger items. However, Bonnie usually bought Jennie lots of smaller gifts. Jennie squealed every year when she got her annual new tin of Crayola Crayons. She loved to color. Whether it was a necklace, new pajamas or a knick-knack, Jennie always acted as if she had just gotten the best gift ever. We never had to worry about Jennie being displeased with whatever she received.

To Jennie, the biggest thing about Christmas is being with family. Other than celebrating the birth of Christ, the next important thing about Christmas was being with grandparents, aunts and uncles and cousins. Especially cousins. Also, Christmas had to include making Christmas candy. The specialties were peanut brittle and chocolate peanut clusters. Christmas could not be Christmas without the sticky process of preparing the brittle. Bonnie and Jennie love that time of bonding. Robbie and I love the eating part a little better!

The fondest memories come from those times when all the kids were little. The Christmas tree would be "swamped" with presents that overflowed into the living room. At both sides of our family, the "drill" was the same. Opening began with the youngest and moved to the oldest. Wrapping paper and bows would fly everywhere! Order soon disintegrated into total chaos as we starting going out of turn. Then we would enjoy a great meal of turkey or roast beef, mashed potatoes, broccoli casserole, rolls, pumpkin and pecan pie and more.

When you lose a loved one, you quickly realize that the things that make Christmas so special when a person is alive makes it a nightmare when they are gone.

The sights, sounds and smells of Christmas serve as constant reminders that someone is missing. One of the coping techniques for grieving families is to radically change their Christmas traditions. For some, it is a matter of "getting out of Dodge." But where can you go that will make it easier to cope with the Christmas season?

Bonnie, Robb and I decided that for this first Christmas without Jennie we would have an "unChristmas." Obviously, we wanted to celebrate the birth of Christ, but decided not to put up a Christmas tree, did not exchange gifts, did not play Christ- mas music and planned to meet friends in Chicago for Christmas Day. The best laid plans of man, however . . .

All of our plans began to change when our friends called and told us that Steve had to work. It was a rare opportunity to get overtime during the holiday season. Then, due to a major snow storm, there was no possibility to get to Chicago by any means of transportation. And there went the "Great Escape!" We called our families and ask if we could join them for Christmas. They opened their arms to all three of us.

Although the meals were delicious, it hurt to have one less plate on the table. Surprisingly, I made it through pretty well during the time we spent with my side of the family. My niece Mendy had gotten married to her husband Tomy just two days after Jennie died. When I called my sister Judy to tell her of Jennie's passing, I asked if they would burn a candle at the wedding in Jennie's honor. Judy quickly agreed.

On Christmas Eve, my extended family did not exchange gifts. Instead, we played "dirty Santa," where you try to keep hold of inexpensive gifts. At the end of our fun, Mendy gave Bonnie a little sack with tissue paper in it. The bag contained the "Jennie candle" that was used at their wedding. My wife is so strong, but Bonnie lost her composure for a few minutes. Somehow, the reality of Jennie's absence hit her through this precious gift.

My moment came during the drive down to Bonnie's side of the family. I experienced "flashbacks" of some of the most difficult moments of Jennie's illness and death. In my mind's eye, I could see Jennie in so much pain as we rushed her to the hospital. Although I had a lifetime of wonderful memories with my daughter, I could not think of anything but the pain of her loss.

A Day of Remembrance

The first memorial Day

THIS MAY SOUND strange, but I *enjoy* visiting cemeteries. My interest in cemeteries was piqued during the summer following eighth-grade. It was at that time that I became my hometown's official bugler for military services. My responsibility was to play "Taps" immediately following the Honor Guard's twenty-one gun salute. Actually, that is not quite accurate. More correctly, I was the *echo bugler* for military services in my hometown.

Royce Junghanns was the official bugler of Medford. I was his echo effect. While standing near the gravesite, Royce would play the first phrase of "Taps," then I would repeat the phrase from a remote location somewhere on the cemetery premises. My unique role required me to stay hidden when the crowd began to gather at the graveside. There is no sense being a visible echo! The artiste in me required a surprise element for this special moment.

My favorite place to situate myself was *in* one of the red cedar trees at the cemetery. I could see out, but it was hard for people to spot me. This concept worked very well until after one service, I walked over to where my dad was talking to someone. Dad began to introduce me to the gentlemen when he noticed that a bird had dropped something white on my light blue jack- et. Dad flicked it off, but my dignity had already been shattered. That may have been the end of my bugling career.

But with all that time hiding in the cemetery, I began to become fascinated with the different gravestones. There was so much interesting information on each marker, plus they were all so different. Therefore, when our family would go to Caldwell, Kansas or Lamont, Oklahoma to decorate family member's graves, I could usually be found walking around checking out the stones. Memorial Day was a task that needed to be done. Then, you had the rest of the day to yourself. That is, until this year—May 30, 2011.

My dad called to see if I knew when our family was going to the cemetery to visit Jennie's grave. The plan was to coordinate our visit so that Mom and Dad could join us. Bonnie had already told me that emotionally she was not ready to visit Jennie's grave again. For me, I needed to go. Robb was planning on joining me, so we set the time as 11:30 a.m. at Perkin's Restaurant in Ponca City. Robb and I were nearly an hour late, but my parents graciously forgave us.

Two significant things happened that day. First, Robb told Dad that he had just watched *Band of Brothers*, a World War II movie. As Robb began asking questions, Dad began telling more war stories than I had heard in my lifetime. I had become familiar with Dad's marksmanship medal, but I never knew that Dad was the first one in his company to finish the grueling course. Because he was so buff, Dad was chosen to carry the ammunition while on the battlefield. Although he was third in line when his group was on the move, he was also in the most dangerous position if he got hit. Their conversation went on for more than an hour! I could have summed up what I knew about Dad's war experience in five minutes before that time.

On the way to the cemetery, we passed the Pioneer Woman statue and museum. Dad began to talk about when he had performed the role of the little boy holding onto the hand of a woman playing the Pioneer Woman. Mom could not believe I had never heard that story. She had heard it more often than necessary.

The second significant thing happened at the cemetery itself. I had seen Jennie's Angel marker before, but today I noticed the dirt that needed to be swept off and the bird droppings that made me wish I had brought a wet paper towel. The reality of Jennie's death hit me again. Then, Dad asked Robb to lead our small family in prayer. Robb prayed a beautiful prayer, then Dad, then Mom and finally me. That which had once been an act of duty became a short worship service. My parents had brought some flowers which we placed next to Jennie's marker. Dad positioned two stakes alongside the potted plant so that it would not fall over. We stood in silence for a little bit. Then Dad said, "Do you remember when Jennie and Meemaw played 'Hide and Seek'?" My mom was always known as "Meemaw" to her grandkids.

Dad did not have to tell the rest of the story. Jennie was probably six or seven when she begged Mom to play the game. As Jennie began to count to ten, Mom took off for the best hiding place she could find. She found a spot in one of the back bedrooms and settled in. Unfortunately, Jennie got distracted by a television program before she finished her countdown.

About thirty minutes later, Mom came out of hiding and into the dining room. She asked, "Where's Jennie?" I told her that Jennie was in the den watching television. Mom said, "I've been hiding from her in the bedroom all this time." As much as Jennie wanted to play, she forgot the *Seeking* part of the game. We all had a good laugh. Robb and I made a short visit to Gammy's grave and then we shared some hugs with each other, got back in the car and headed back to town.

I know this may sound like a fairly simple day, but I needed that time to share my grief with my parents. We had not had that private time alone to face what had happened. Something very meaningful happened for me in those three or four hours. God brought a new source of comfort.

I will never see Memorial Day in the same way again. The miles and time it takes to get to the cemetery are well worth it.

Was it a Morning Like This

The First Easter

EASTER IS: THE Empty Tomb, the Resurrected Christ, Hope for all mankind, pretty little girls dressed up in new dresses, Easter eggs hunts, Sunrise services, a day of celebration. How could anyone find it difficult to "survive" Easter? For our family, Easter 2011 was challenging in many ways. Although it ended up being the best Easter we have ever experienced, it did not seem as if it would be.

If it was a baseball game, our family would have faced Easter with three strikes against us. It fell on April 24th in 2011. That usually wouldn't have mattered, but Jennie's birthday is April 21st. The first strike was dealing with Jennie's first birthday apart just three days before Easter Sunday. We had celebrated Jennie's thirty-second birthday with such grandeur. A year ago, we had hope that God would do another miracle in Jennie's life. Now, we faced the reality of her death with a huge hole in our hearts. The day just brought fresh memories of her loss.

The second strike was Easter Sunday itself. Bonnie had always made a "big deal" out of Easter for the kids. There were Easter baskets waiting for them when they woke up. Then, there was the traditional photo of Jennie and Robbie in new outfits for Easter Sunday. Robb would always look a little uncomfortable in his new suit and tie. Jennie would wear a new frilly dress with white patent shoes and lacey socks. Most years, we did Easter egg hunts and the usual traditional activities.

Jennie had added one new tradition to her list: Promise of Hope. For seven years, our church had presented an Easter pageant called Promise of Hope. The church was turned into a first-century Jewish setting with costumes, make-up, smoke machines, an amazing, complex set and even animals. The only missing element we could never get to work was a donkey for the Triumphal Entry. The one year we attempted a more realistic entry for Jesus, the donkey took two steps into the sanctuary, sat down on his haunches and began to bray at the top of his voice. Fortunately, it was at a practice.

Jennie loved Promise of Hope! She was only able to be in the presentation one year, because we discontinued it the next year. Still, Jennie poured herself into the production with all of her heart. Nobody invited more friends, sang from the depth of their heart or put as much energy into her character as Jennie. She was a natural-born actress and clown to begin with, but she loved telling the story of Jesus' Death and Resurrection.

The third strike was that Easter Sunday 2011 was my last Sunday in the pastorate. After thirty-three years of pastoring, I felt it was time to "retire" from my present pastorate and pursue a different avenue of ministry. I wept openly the day that I made the announcement to the congregation back in January 2011. From the time I was called to preach at sixteen, I had always planned to pastor for forty years and then retire. When I was twenty-five, that was "the plan" every ministerial student had when they graduated college or Seminary. Now, I found myself in the awkward position of falling seven years short of my goal. A 58-year-old pastor is not exactly "hot property." I have always believed that if you are not where you are comfortable at fifty, any pastor is going to face some difficult days.

So what do you do when you are down-in-the-count before you pick up the bat? You pull out all the stops and swing away! I have already told you about Jennie's birthday celebration 2011, but listen to this finish: an Easter weekend with not one, but two concerts with Sandi Patty! Every pastor wants to see the church full on Easter Sunday, but what about two "sold-out" performances. That is exactly what happened!

My friend, John Bond, had wanted to do something to honor Jennie on a permanent basis. He actually did several things in that regard, but John's idea was to begin a concert series in Jennie's honor. I even gave it a title: Angel Touch Ministries. As we thought of who the first artist might be, we agreed on Sandi Patty. Jennie loved Sandi Patty's music. Jennie had even sung with Sandi on stage at the Fox Theatre in Detroit when Jennie was little. She was not a child prodigy. She went up on stage for the "Friend Company" portion of the concert. Jennie never forgot that moment.

I called Sandi's agent to book a date. I knew we needed some time to advertise, so I asked the agent if they had any availability in April.

Although Easter Sunday seemed like an impossibility, the weekend was open! I booked it immediately, I do not know who was more excited, John or me. He was so excited that he booked a second concert the Saturday beforehand. If I'm going to retire, might as well have "the Voice" sing me out, right?

On Wednesday, April 20, 2011, Sandi Patty was honored at the beginning of the Dove Awards with a presentation with the nominees for Female Vocalist of the Year singing a medley of Sandi Patty "hits." We watched the delayed telecast on Easter Sunday night. Sandi humbly told me it was "no big deal." I do not think it was my imagination when I heard most of the nominees singing with a little "fear" in their voice. At the close of that portion of the Doves, Sandi walked on stage to join the nominees. I thought to myself, "Ladies, you are going hear how it is done!" The legendary Ms. Patty lit up the stage. Later that night, she was awarded her 40th Dove Award, more than anyone else in the industry.

Bonnie and I were present at Sandi Patty's first solo concert in Wichita, Kansas years before. The concert was held in a large venue with a sold-out crowd. Later we saw her with our children in Detroit, Michigan at the historic Fox Theatre. We usually needed binoculars to see who was on stage. The sanctuary at Bartlesville First Church of the Nazarene is very beautiful, but comfortably holds 700 people. What if on my last Easter Sunday we had to turn people away from service? Although we did not face that problem, I did fantasize about telling people, "I am sorry, you cannot come to our church today." What could anyone do to me? Only kidding!

Because they are always there when we need them, our friends, Steve and Beth Boyce, flew in from Flint, Michigan for Jennie's birthday and the Easter weekend. Their presence has always made good times better and bad times bearable. Although we all are fans of Sandi, our friend Beth may be the biggest fan Sandi Patty has!

On Saturday April 23, 2011, I stood next to the piano and told Sandi a short version of Jennie's story. I had already sent a couple of chapters from this book to Sandi to read for background. With all the excitement and honor she had experienced just three days earlier, Sandi wanted to know about Jennie. That night, Sandi dedicated "We Shall Behold Him" in Jennie's honor. Although there were plenty of standing ovations throughout the concert, I will always remember that moment.

On Easter Sunday morning, the concert began with a beautiful video tribute to Jennie. Once again, "We Shall Behold Him" was sung in Jennie's honor. I told the congregation I had to believe that Jesus and Jennie had taken their seats to enjoy this service to the fullest. The moment I will remember most from that service was when I went up to take the offering. Sandi went down and sat next to Bonnie. It was not a ministry of song, but of presence that Bonnie needed desperately.

Have you ever experienced a "perfect ending?" I did that day! It was more than the crowd or the music, as wonderful as that was. The Holy Spirit came! I felt affirmed in the choices I had made. Like a cleansing stream, so much pain and doubt was just washed away! I so needed that. I could leave a calling I had known for over forty years with my head up and my heart full!

After the service, Bonnie and Beth had a great time talking and laughing with Sandi. Those three young ladies were having way too much fun. It was like they had known each other forever. It was so good to see Bonnie laugh after she had known so many tears. I was glad to see her experience joy even for a brief moment.

For me, the most meaningful moment happened at the front door of the church. My farewell reception had been held on April 17, 2011. It was a lovely day that included a delicious meal, generous gifts and a good-hearted "roast." The only problem I had was that I really did not get to say a proper good-bye to so many people. The day was busy. The Family Life Center was pretty crowded. I just needed time to give some hugs and tell people that I loved them.

The "perfect ending" came as people stopped at the front door. I had that sacred moment to experience a flood of memories of how God had worked in so many lives. There was no evening service, so we could take as much time as we needed. Each time a person or family stepped up, I was reminded of the "stories" God had written in their lives the past eleven years. There were college students that I had known since they were little children and high school students who were barely out of kindergarten when I first met them. There were young families who I had walked with through several major milestones in their life: their first date, the excitement of their engagement, officiating at their wedding and dedicating their children. There were Senior Adults who had experienced the loss of their children, health problems and the loss of a spouse. There were good friends that I will not see as often, because life has a way of moving on. There were people I would never see again! The ones that brought me the most tears were the little boys and girls that I had known since birth.

I have come to believe that all that is left when a pastor retires are the stories that God has written throughout their ministry. No one will care what size church you pastored or how many building programs you completed. All retired preachers have left are the memories of how God moved to change lives, plus a thousand corny jokes!

The Last First

The First anniversary of Jennie's death

IT IS 9:48 p.m. on June 17, 2011 . . . the last first . . . the anniversary of Jennie's death. No one really celebrates this anniversary. You mark it. Another milestone that you survived!

Bonnie's family all met at the chicken place in Okarche, Oklahoma. It was a good, short drive. It was something to do instead of staying home. On the drive, we were able to see some of the damage that had been caused by a recent tornado in Piedmont. We tried to keep the conversation light. It was still hard to laugh without feeling guilty.

I would summarize our approach to this last milestone as avoidance. We tried to fill our day with activities that would keep our mind off of the "elephant in the room." I'm not sure that is the proper way to mark the first anniversary of a death, but it was the only way we knew to survive.

The first anniversary of a loved one's death is hard because it dredges up negative memories that are better left forgotten. I could picture in my mind's eye Jennie standing in our house screaming in pain and desperation. The moment after we got the news about the reality of Jennie dying echoed through my mind with a freshness that I did not want or need. I realized again how desperately we all missed her.

When I am hurting, I get really quiet. I do not cover up my emotions very well either. Bonnie and Robbie always know when something is bothering me. I am silent because I am processing my emotions. I was very quiet on this anniversary. The fried chicken and okra did not distract me for very long.

I had come to a place in the healing process where there were more good memories than bad, but I suffered a major setback that day. It did not last very long, but the memories made for a very miserable time.

175

In many ways, I thought I would be further than this after a year. I was sure I would have this book completed, but I came to realize that the story has more facets than I originally thought. It is also harder to write than I thought. Not so much hard to tell, but hard to be concise. What do people want to know? What is excessive detail? When I write, I always "talk too much."

My emotions have been on a roller coaster ride throughout these last six months. I thought it would not hurt anymore, but it will always hurt! A year ago, I was finding it hard to get up in the morning. Today, I just never know when it is going to hit me. I was driving home from the chicken place with Baba. I started thinking about Jennie and got weepy-eyed. Sometimes, I need to pull over to get myself together.

On one trip home to Edmond from Bartlesville, I wept for two and a half hours straight. I feel like I need to apologize every time my voice breaks or tears begin to flow. People are patient, but I am sure many think my family's recovery should be completed by now. After all, it has been a year!

On the anniversary, I wanted to drive up to the cemetery to visit Jennie's grave. Even though I had been there on Memorial Day with my parents and Robbie, I thought it would be fitting to make another trip to "see" her. Bonnie was not emotionally ready to do so. I am not sure I was either, but it seemed like a good idea mentally. In the end, none of us went to Longwood Cemetery that day. In fact, none of us have been back since Memorial Day. Those visits will come . . . just not today.

We tried very hard to not dwell on Jennie's death that day, but to be quite honest, some of those horrible memories of watching her die flooded my mind and heart again. I knew better than to open a discussion about what I was feeling, because the floodgates would open for all of us.

I went to see my new doctor a few days ago. After sharing a little about Jennie's death, the doctor asked me, "Do you have anyone to talk to about what you are feeling?" I realized how much I missed my visits with John Bond. Being in a new place is great in many ways, but it can also be lonely. It is hard to sit down with a new friend and open up. I will get there, but right now, most of my emotions have to be bottled up.

I realized that Bonnie is in the same boat. We have not been able to have a good talk about our loss yet. It hurts too much. It breaks my heart to hear her weep. Instead, she has gathered her family around her as a source of comfort and support. This is the first time since her sister was a senior in High School that Bonnie and Jenarold have lived in the same city.

Robb is busy with school and teaching, but I know he has been covering his emotions in order to protect us. He has stayed strong for us. I appreciate his compassion and care, but I also know he will have to find an outlet for what he is feeling inside.

We love being closer to members of both sides of the family. It is a real joy to watch Kaitlin, Kenzie, Michael, Mariah, Rachel, Henry, Annabelle and Cayden grow up. We are able to get more "glimpses" of Hannah and Wyatt plus Daniel and Shantal. We even have Truett, Kannon and Mr./ Miss Stanford on the way! Still, I am reminded of how much Jennie would enjoy being here. It will get better, I know. Just not yet!

Bridges Over Troubled Water

Tug of War

Day breaks, and heartaches fill your morning with sadness. If you'd
let go, you'd soon know that God can fill your life with gladness.

You're acting like Jonah, and there's a price that you'll pay
if you follow your own road instead of God's way.

He wants to lead you here, but you pull there.
It's a tug of war, and you're not getting anywhere.

You can shout and fight with all your might, but you'll never really win.
So why don't you confess your sins?

And just settle for second place in the tug of war.

In Grave Condition

THE WEEK BEFORE Jennie went into the hospital, I was teaching a Pastoral Care Class at Oklahoma Wesleyan University. We had reached the Death and Dying portion of the class. This made me remember that preachers and funeral directors have very twisted senses of humor. The funny things that happen at funerals can be unbelievable.

I once did a funeral for a family I had only met the day before. As the hearse pulled out of the driveway of the funeral home, I looked back just in time to see the hearse's back door fly open and then shut again quickly. We were on one of the busier streets in Flint, Michigan. I was riding with the Funeral Director in the lead vehicle. When I told him what I had just seen, he first denied that it could have happened and then admitted, "We have been having a little trouble with that door latch."

The main thing holding a casket in a hearse is a metal plate on the hearse floor—and the back door. We had come very close to dumping a casket into pretty heavy traffic. Of course, the family car was right behind the hearse. Instead of stopping, the Funeral Director drove on to the cemetery. As I was preparing to lead the casket to the gravesite, the wife and daughter of the deceased ran to the Funeral Director shouting, "You will be meeting our lawyer first thing on Monday!" Fortunately, it was Saturday, so he had plenty of time to get out of town.

I tell you that story to prepare you for the fact that my presentation of funerals and dealing with loss was not exactly reverent. I always told the story about the Funeral Home Organist who died during a service. Of course, when she fell forward, the weight of her body caused dozens of organ keys to play all at once. The staff had to jerk the woman's body (who was the Funeral Home Director's mother-in-law) out of the organ room. They went right on with the funeral as if nothing had happened.

181

I also told how a Funeral Home had exhumed the casket of a 21-year-old mother who died giving birth in order to move her body to Ohio. Just out of curiosity, the Funeral Home opened the casket to check their work. After twenty-one years in the ground, the young woman's body was in "great" shape. The Funeral Home called the husband and son and asked the son, "Would you like to see what your Mother looked like when she was your age?" The young man flew down from Ohio, saw his Mom at twenty-one and flew back to his home.

It might help you to understand if I told you that one of my lessons was entitled, "The First Word in Funeral is Fun!" One of my favorite classes during this module was "The Seven Stages of Dying." I always showed a clip from an episode of a television show called *Monk*. The episode is entitled *Monk Finds a New Psychiatrist*. Dr. Kroger decides to retire, and tells Monk he will no longer be able to see him. At that point, Monk goes through the Seven Stages of Grief three times in three minutes. Natalie asks Dr. Kroger what is happening. He responds, "This is denial; that is anger; then acceptance . . ."

Little did I know that before the next week was out, I would not be laughing at all. Fortunately for me, God gave me a friend who walked with me over what he called "the bridges" of sorrow. Let me introduce you to my friend John and the lessons I am learning as we walk together.

Special Agent 007

HIS NAME IS Bond . . . John Bond! Unlike the secret agent of movie fame, this Bond does not drive an Aston Martin, an Alfa Romeo or a Lotus. He drives a Durango. As far as I know, John does not have any poisonous gadgets or special communication devices. Whereas James was known to be arrogant and cocky, John is a humble servant of God. James Bond loved the spotlight. John Bond is happiest when he is unnoticed. John's greatest brush with danger is when a computer "crashes." The one similarity between the two men would be that both men usually will be found wearing a dark suit.

When John and his wife Joyce first started attending the church where I pastored, they would slip into service very quietly. I am not sure I would have noticed them that first Sunday had it not been for their good friend, Dottie Goard. Dottie had known John and Joyce for over twenty years. Although Dottie was fairly new to our congregation, she enthusiastically invited her friends to join her. A couple of days after the Bond's first visit, Dottie called me at the church office to tell me how blessed we were to have the Bonds with us. She spent several minutes telling me the good things she knew about them. After getting to know John and Joyce, I would have to agree that it would be difficult to find two finer Christian people.

Although we had been on some church outings together, I did not get to know John and Joyce well until we took a Spanish class together at the church. Studies have usually come easily for me, but that Spanish class was a struggle. I missed a few sessions then completely lost my way when we started into grammar. By comparison, one of the members of our class knew Spanish so well that he was pointing out mistakes in the textbook.

His mastery of the Spanish language did not bother me so much. I was just a newbie. How could I be expected to meet such a high standard of excellence? All I remembered from sixth-grade Spanish was *Casa Bonita*—beautiful house. I would have forgotten that except that it was the name of one of my favorite Mexican restaurants! I found comfort in the fact that most beginners were having problems. I rationalized that it was impossible for anyone to pick up this foreign language where "*i*" is pronounced "*e*."

Trips to Lowes became a part of my routine. My focus was not on power tools or lumber; I went to practice pronouncing the Spanish equivalents that were below all the English signs. Our teacher, LeeAnn Lopez, was very patient with me, but my greatest battle was over correct pronunciation. I could roll my "R's" very well, but everything else sounded like gibberish coming out of my mouth. If it was impossible to learn Spanish, that meant it would be a superhuman act to just pronounce it, right? I was convinced no one could accomplish such a great task.

Then there was Joyce. She had never studied Spanish, but she was getting it. Her vocabulary was growing stronger each week. She was excelling at comprehension of the grammar. To add insult to injury, Joyce spoke the words as if she had grown up in Mexico City. Spanish seemed to "flow" from her lips. How amazing, yet how discouraging for me.

Surely, Joyce had more time on her hands than I did. After all, I was a pastor. Preparing sermons, counseling people in need, board meetings and so on kept me busy. Joyce must be at home each day quietly studying without interruption. Once again, my excuse was stripped away when I realized that Joyce worked full-time with John at their own thriving business. I had to face it; Joyce was a better student than I was. Whenever I would complement her on her progress, she would just shyly smile and thank me.

Although it was obvious that both John and Joyce were leaders, they would politely decline any "upfront" type of positions. They believed they could best serve "behind the scenes." They helped at an Easter community outreach event. They did not mind getting sweaty. Touching lives for Christ was a part of who they were. When I was invited to their company Christmas banquet this year, I realized what a large ministry they have within their business. It is clear that John and Joyce loved their employees, and that the Bonds are loved as well.

It was around Thanksgiving in 2009 that I received a phone call from the church telling me that Joyce had died in a tragic drowning accident in Tennessee. While trying to winterize a boat with John, Joyce fell into the water. Unable to swim, and possibly unconscious before she hit the water, Joyce didn't even flounder. John dove in immediately, but to no avail.

John himself suffered a heart attack while trying to pull his wife to shore. Joyce's loss was amplified by how close she was to her husband. They were inseparable. I do not remember seeing them apart from each other.

As he began to grieve, I was amazed at how strong John appeared to be on the outside. Although he suffered a heart attack, John waited to see a doctor until a more convenient time. Even though it meant long hours and great stress, John made sure the needs of his employees were met. His busy schedule did not allow him to think of himself very often. He had to be reminded to go to the doctor. From my present vantage point, I wish I could have understood the pain that existed behind John's smile. I tried to do a good job at the funeral. I tried to keep in contact with John on occasion. I know I prayed for him, but I had no idea how excruciating the loss was to him.

Until Jennie died, I did not understand the devastating pain that comes after the funeral is over. Unless you have experienced such a loss, you cannot understand the emotions. It is a natural course of life for people to get back to "normal." Life goes on. It has to! In fact, the majority of people will expect you to bounce back fairly quickly as well. As much as I hate to admit it, I have been guilty of the same expectations of others. I never understood why my Great Aunt Fern cried over the loss of Uncle Charlie at every family Thanksgiving dinner for thirty years.

So where do you turn when your heart has been torn apart?

Bonnie and I met with grief counselors for a couple of weeks, but it just did not seem to reach the hurt. A few months after Jennie's death, I was consumed by the loss. Instead of healing all things, time was intensifying my pain. During that horrible time, I received a letter from John Bond. It was not your usual sympathy card. It was a letter from John offering to walk with me during my time of grief.

John wrote about "bridges" that he had crossed since Joyce had died. He did not claim to have finished his journey of grief, but shared that he was a "few steps" ahead of me. He offered to meet with me weekly, just to be there for me. We agreed to meet every Wednesday at 2:30 p.m. at Braum's, a wonderful ice cream store. We developed a pretty good routine each week.

2:30 p.m. Pick-up at the church

2:33 p.m. Park at Braums, always in the first parking space on the SW corner

2:34 p.m. Place ice cream order (double-dip pistachio almond for John, double strawberry sundae with nuts for me).

2:35-3:30 p.m. Talk about life.

3:30 p.m. Head back to the church.

3:35 p.m. John would lay his hand on my shoulder and pray for me. The prayer would always end by saying, "And everyone said . . . Amen!"

Throughout our journey together, John did a lot of listening. Sometimes, it was very difficult for me to speak. John let me talk, cry and vent. John is a very generous man, but the greatest gift he gave to me is his presence. Just being there is so important when someone is hurting. John never used a white board or even a pen and napkin. He just walked with me.

I am not sure that I could give a formal outline of the *bridges* that we crossed together, but I do want to share some of those crossings that my family experienced, and give a word picture that illustrates that experience. No one crosses these bridges just once. I have found myself having to re-cross some bridges numerous times. In the eighth and ninth month following Jennie's death, I experienced pain almost as intense as the first month. That bridge takes a long time to get over.

I owe John great thanks for being that "one who sticks closer than a brother." His presence has been used as a healing agent. We will be friends for life. Braums any time . . . just call and I will be there.

The Bridge of Numbness

THE WORD PICTURE that comes to mind is that of a zombie— walking on the outside, but dead on the inside. Immediately after Jennie died, we all went into a shock that got us through the day of the funeral. We were surrounded by family and friends. The Celebration Service was exactly how we wanted Jennie to be remembered. We smiled and even laughed as we remembered how Jennie's life had touched us. Marching out of the sanctuary was like a victory parade. It was thoroughly a Jennie-type thing to do.

When our family and friends had to go re-enter their world, the reality of Jennie's loss began to set in. At least for me, my initial reaction was not intense emotions as much as a numbness that left me almost emptied of any emotions. I could not feel anything. I was just lost. The ability to smile or laugh was gone. I could not find a place of solace anywhere. Bonnie and Robb were hurting as much as I was. None of us were ready to open up about what we were feeling. What do you do when you realize that you have to pick up the pieces of your life? Why couldn't we just wake up and have this all be a bad dream?

Some friends offered to let us use their discount on a cabin in Branson, Missouri. It seemed like it would be a good idea to get away for a few days. When we got to the cabin, we all sat down and looked at each other. It seemed that we had just moved our grief to a different location. It was raining outside, but I did not want to stay in the cabin. I wanted to find a place to run and hide. Somewhere safe, somewhere that would make the emptiness go away.

We drove back from Branson no better than when we left. As I mentioned before, I had been *out of the pulpit* since Jennie was taken to the hospital that night in early April. Now, it was time to step back into my responsibilities. Because I was so numb, it was impossible for me to "shake hands and be friendly" like Brother Staley admonished us when I was a kid. I walked as quickly as I could to my office. I waited to come out until most people had left. I could not even fake a smile, much less carry on a conversation.

It is hard for a pastor to be emotionless. I think people see pastors as a little like Santa Claus—always jolly, always *up*, always concerned about the congregation more than themselves. To be that person on a good day can sometimes be hard. If people have a complaint about anything, the pastor usually hears about it. We get tattled to a lot. "Pastor, you know what Fred did to me? What are you going to do about it?" It is not a scientifically-proven fact, but 95% of the phone calls a pastor receives are about something somebody needs *from* you. The other 5% are wrong numbers.

Most of the first two months, I felt like a zombie. Nothing brought me joy or relief. I tried to get up every morning and make it through the day. People were good to try to be understanding, but they did not understand what was going on in my heart, or in Bonnie and Robb's hearts. They couldn't. I know our family and friends would have done anything to take the pain away, but that was never possible.

I also found myself seeking Robbie. Robb had moved over to Jennie's house for the time being. When I got home, I would look for him in our house and then hurry over to Jennie's. I would panic if I could not find him immediately. I wanted to make sure he was safe. I wouldn't talk much, but I just wanted to be able to see him. I only had one child left. I could not bear the idea of losing him. Robb was fine, but my fear was as real as if he were in danger.

I was too broken to be much help to Bonnie. Being a Pastor's Wife is much like being a Pastor, but with your hands tied behind your back. Bonnie experienced her own pain, *plus* mine.

She knew how hard it was for me, but was powerless to step in. She could not take my place in a Board Meeting or preach a sermon for me. She just hugged me and sent me "off to the battle."

There is always stress at church, but now the congregation was grieving Jennie's death and to a great degree the loss of their pastor and his family, plus two staff members leaving to take pastorates. In the midst of the void that my absence had created, it seemed like nothing was settled. It felt like free-falling without a parachute. If I had to do it all over again, I would have taken off my "Pastor's Mask" more and not tried to act like I was all right. I should have seized the opportunity to help people understand the grieving process. Being a people-pleaser, I tried to be the pastor that I thought the congregation needed.

There was a great deal of compassion shown to our family. The majority of people tried their best to be patient and understanding. There are no *right words* during times like this, but most of us are afraid of saying the *wrong thing*, so we do not say anything at all. Hugs are a universal language of love. If you do not know what to say, a hug will speak volumes. People who needed to talk with me about their lives were sensitive to the fact that "now was not a good time." As is always true, there were some who expected more out of me than I could give. Declining attendance, casting vision, hiring new staff, keeping finances up—none of that mattered to me. It only made it worse to realize I was not *leading* the church.

I really tried to muster up the strength to fix the church. No one wanted things to go back to normal more than I did. There were just no magical answers. It seemed the harder I tried, the worse it got.

As bad as the numbness felt, it would prove to be better than when the numbness began to wane a little. Like having your gums numbed at a dentist, there comes a time when the pain hits full-force.

The Bridge of Anger

THE WORD PICTURE I would use for this bridge is a teapot just about to whistle. There is something boiling inside which is about to explode. Of all the bridges, this has been the most difficult one to cross for me. The main reason is that I do not want to admit this bridge exists. I want it to be invisible to everyone, including myself.

I grew up in a fairly legalistic stage of Church history. I am not sure it was actually stated, but I drew the conclusion that God's love was based on "Do's" and "Don't's." In fact, as a teenager, I would have answered how I knew I was a Christian by listing the things I didn't do far more than the things I did. Let me pause for just a moment to let some of you say, "Amen!"

Along with many vices that were to be avoided, there was also an unrealistic expectation that Christians never get mad or angry. We had Sunday School lessons that emphasized the evil of losing your temper. There are two standard responses to that: Defeat, or Denial. Defeat came when you got angry, admitted it and gave up. I was sure only backsliders did that. Denial came when you got angry, did not admit it and covered it up.

Denial became an art form for me. Of course, I frequently used the phrase, "Righteous Indignation" and cited Jesus' cleansing of the Temple. Everyone knew that Jesus was not angry; He was indignant, and rightfully so. I also added my own twist to things when I excused my actions by explaining that I was frustrated, not angry. Everyone gets frustrated at times. This approach worked for me most of my adolescent years, into my young adulthood.

When I became a pastor, I added the factor that I was "God's anointed." You cannot always lose an argument when you say, "Do not come against God's anointed!" It took me a while to admit I experienced anger, and even longer to realize I needed to apologize for my attitude once in a while. I was capable of having a bad attitude. My Achilles' heel was when someone criticized my character. Then I felt affirmed in being able to evoke the voice of Moses as he raises His rod at the Red Sea. My Charlton Heston-side came out. I started using phrases like, "Thou knowest not," or "Thence forth thou shallest . . ."

With that concept of anger, I really faced a problem when Jennie died, because I could never be angry at God. I even told Him, "I am not angry at You, just confused and hurt."

I would not admit that I was angry at some people who had hurt me. I thought I had done an exceptional job of hiding my true emotions. Hiding your anger is like trying to deny that there is a gob of food stuck between your teeth. Every time you open your mouth, everybody knows!

I decided to leave the pastorate. In preparation for my transition out, I applied for a CPE—Clinical Pastoral Education— class held at Deaconess Hospital in Oklahoma City. The class was held on Wednesdays, beginning in January 2011. I drove down to interview with CPE instructor, Ken Blank. He told me that this would be a community-based CPE course requiring something called verbatims and preaching. Ken accepted me into the program. I drove home thinking, "This is going to be a breeze." After all, I had a doctorate in Community Ministries and preaching was one of my strengths.

When the class started, I realized that we were a "small group." I hate small groups, because you have to talk and be open. I am also good at avoiding being involved in a small group. I am an expert in being able to turn the focus away from me. I just become a good listener. Ask a couple of questions and keep someone else talking. It worked, too—until I preached the second week of class.

I used a sermon on forgiveness that I had preached a couple of weeks before. In order to keep everyone from writing a critique, I gave away my sermon outline by giving three key words to the class. I thought I did a good job of teaching about our need to forgive others. I sat down and waited for the evaluations. I had great feedback. Good presentation! Way to go! The class even said they would come back and hear me preach if they had a chance.

I sat down and thought, "Whew! That is over!" I was a little nervous, but I did okay.

Then someone asked, "Why are you so angry?"

I was shocked! I am not angry. I do not get angry! I asked them to explain.

Someone said, "When you talked about some of those people, you seemed angry."

I muddled through a quick excuse and survived the last hour.

I thought, "Why would they think I am angry at anyone? Just because I raised my voice and got red in the face a few times does not mean I am angry. Emotional maybe, but not angry. Besides, I had a good reason to be angry if I really was—but I am not angry."

I succeeded in keeping other people talking until one week, when it felt like the whole class "turned on me." They wanted to address my anger and talk about forgiveness. "Wait a minute. Let's talk about you!" They kept trying to pry open the door to my special hiding place.

I had an interview for a Resident Chaplain position at a nearby hospital a few weeks later. I thought I would slip out for the interview and be done for the day. Ken asked me to come back after the interview and share how it went. I did not really want to do that, but I wanted to be compliant.

I walked into the interview with five of the nicest chaplains you would ever want to meet. We chatted for a few minutes. The director asked, "Are you ready for the interview?"

I thought, "Sure, fire away!"

The first question was, "Why is someone like you applying for this job?"

I began to stutter and stammer, "Well, my daughter died in June and—"

The Director quickly asked, "I understand that your daughter died. I do, but why is someone who has had three long successful pastorates applying for this job? What is the reason, really? There has to be something deeper than that. Are you angry at God? Or is it a person that you are upset with?" Had this committee been talking to my CPE director? Not fair!

What happened next completely took me off-guard. I began to confess every reason in the world why I was angry. I told them things I would only reveal to my family. I named names! Have you ever had a moment when you wish you could stop talking, but your mouth seemed out of control? I ended up in a puddle on the floor. They had me tell Jennie's story and were very compassionate, but the one compliment I came away with was, "You are a good writer."

All I wanted to do was go home and crawl in bed. I even wondered if Ken and the other three students would notice if I did not go back. Being the "rule keeper" that I am, I knew I had to return to class.

Everybody anxiously asked, "How did it go?" "Terrible," I said, "They said I was . . . angry!"

The class sat quietly stunned. It was one of those awkward moments similar to falling down and hoping no one noticed. They consoled me. Ken even took extra time the next week to encourage me.

Okay, my cover has been blown, but I will recover my disguise. They will forget about it, I thought. Instead, Ken started teaching the class about "non-anxious responses." The bottom line was to keep your composure when someone has hurt you, and do not seek revenge. I have always prided myself in being a good student, but this did not compute.

Ken started speaking a foreign language to me. I had struggled to admit I was angry to start with. Now, he is telling me there is a better way to handle the situation? In fact, in order to forgive like I had preached about, I needed to learn how to deal with anger without making things worse by responding with such great emotions. I struggled with his message, because I could forgive God and anybody else *after* they were held accountable.

"God, explain Yourself! I am not mad at you, but you better make sense out of Jennie's death—and do it NOW!"

"As soon as I get an apology, even if I have to beat it out of someone, I will let go. I just need to be *right*, and everyone needs to know that I am *right*." Of all things, no one in the class chimed in, "Enough with Randy's problems, let's talk about me!" Where is a good, insensitive egomaniac when you need one?

It took a long time to admit I WAS angry and even longer to admit that I was also *causing* the anger to get worse. I had gotten mad a lot, but never accepted that I had to let it go even if I never got my revenge. What was that I said about unconditional forgiveness? I admitted, "Okay, so I don't practice what I preach."

The hardest bridge for me to cross other than the Perfect Storm has been the Bridge of Anger. I felt like I was being beaten to death in front of everyone's eyes and no one stepped in to stop it. In fact, I doubt that 98% of the people even knew what was going on. If I did not learn to release my bitterness, it was going to impact even my ability to get a job. That is serious.

I would like to say that I took a walk in a garden where God gave me peace that washed my anger away. In reality, I did not find relief until I resigned. When I knew I could not be hurt anymore, I was better. Not completely healed, but better.

That may sound like a bad thing, but here is what is even more peculiar: the pain that I experienced made it easier to let go of my emotions towards pastoring. I did not want to pastor anymore. Ever since I was five years old, I wanted to be a pastor. When I visited my Grandpa Akin, I imagined how wonderful it would be to have people pat you on the back after service, tell you what a great job you did and brag on how much they loved you. I had no idea that he had been voted out of several churches.

When I was seven, our family made the front page of the *Medford Patriot-Star*. I cannot remember why our picture was front page news, but I do remember that underneath the picture the inscription read, "Judy wants to be a teacher. Randy wants to be a preacher." I longed to be called of God.

But for the first-time in my 33 years of ministry, I did not feel any twisted emotions about leaving. I was able to "release the church" without feeling like I had to be the "best pastor they ever had."

I have made every effort not to ask, "How is the church doing?" I have been surprised how much I am enjoying just being "Randy" again. I still enjoy preaching on occasion, but I do not miss it as much as I thought. I have been "unemployed" since Easter Sunday 2011. By the fall of 2011, I have spent my time writing, sipping coffee on the back porch with Bonnie and my father-in-law, sipping Diet Coke with them in the evening as the sun goes down . . . and I've never been happier in my life.

Except when Jennie was with me.

The Bridge of the Perfect Storm

THE WORD PICTURE to describe this bridge is the closing scene from the movie *The Perfect Storm*. The scene features the crew of a fishing boat losing a battle to an overwhelming monster storm at sea. They have been struggling to survive against unbelievable odds, but—I'm going to spoil the ending—now the audience knows they are not going to make it. One by one, the crew drops below the surface of the ocean. They are drowning, unable to breathe and going under.

Likewise, for me, somewhere in the first three months, the pain began to intensify. With tsunami force, the pain and emotions hit me to the point of nearly disabling me. When I made it to the office, I usually just sat at my computer and cried. I tried writing to Jennie as a source of therapy, but every word seemed to open up the wound instead of heal it.

The only way I can describe it is to use the word *torment*. Daily, my mind would be flooded with flashbacks of Jennie's worst moments—standing in the house screaming in pain before we took her to the hospital, her words when we received the diagnosis ("Daddy," she cried, "you said it wouldn't be cancer! I don't want to die!"), the lifeless look on her face those last few weeks—my mind could not free itself from those devastating thoughts.

I think Bonnie knew that if she released her emotions around me, there would be a flood that could not be stopped. I cannot imagine how much she hurt, especially when she was alone. I realize now that Robbie was containing his heartache in order to comfort us. I am not sure we have yet taken the time to allow ourselves to grieve as a couple and as a family.

Instead, we found ways to suppress our grief. I noticed Bonnie started playing Solitaire on her iPhone every night to wear herself out enough to sleep. I could not keep my left hand still or stop grinding my teeth. Robbie picked up on the *twitches* and could tell when I was especially bothered. I could hide my anxiety from most people, but Robb read me like a book.

During this time, I sent an email to many of my pastoral friends which revealed my desperate state. I told them I was seriously considering leaving the pastorate. I was in no emotional state to do anything else, but maybe I could find a job that would make the pain go away. Each one of my friends reminded me not to make any hasty choices. "Be easy on yourself," they said. "You are going to make it!"

Two of those friends were Dr. Jerry Porter and his wife, Toni. Right before Dr. Porter was elected General Superintendent in the Church of the Nazarene, the Porters lost their only daughter to cancer. Their daughter had been preparing to get married. She suffered great pain. Dr. Porter's schedule is unbelievably hectic, but he and Toni were willing to meet us somewhere or allow us to come to their home. Toni talked to Bonnie on the phone.

Bonnie asked Toni, "How long does it take to start healing?" Toni answered, "It took us about three years."

Three years seemed like an eternity. I could not imagine enduring this intense pain for that long. Although we try to find comfort in the healing of time, time does not necessarily bring healing. It certainly does not seem like an ally when you are in the midst of the storm.

I lived in a state of turmoil. I came to a place where I thought it would be impossible to remain in the pastorate past February. My stomach would become knotted just thinking about it. Of course, my indecision kept Bonnie torn up. We had a house payment and would be without health insurance. She encouraged me to stay through Easter.

When I finally realized that I would have to resign for our well-being, and that I needed to quit trying to *fix things*, the intensity began to lessen some. It was like breaking the surface of the water and taking that first breath. I did not know what the future held, but I knew the decision to leave was the right one. Even though I had not seen it yet, I knew the house we were moving to was where we were supposed to be.

If I could share a word of encouragement to those who are crossing the bridge of the perfect storm right now, *it will not always be this way!* The sun will shine again. You will laugh again. You cannot go back to how it was, but you will be able to move forward . . . someday. My Grandma Schuneman had a saying that was not original with her, but has been an anchor for me at times. She would say, "This too shall pass!" And it will.

I would also share a word of advice to those who are dealing with grieving people. You may not understand the emotions that person is going through, but be sensitive to them. If they begin to tear up, stop your conversation and console them. You have hit a nerve! Try as best you can not to use clichés. You do not know how they feel, so do not tell them that you do. Do not try to explain to them God's purpose in all this. If nothing else, just be there. Your presence will bring more healing than you know!

The Bridge of Waves

THE WORD PICTURE for this bridge is *wading in the ocean on a windy day*. It feels so good to get your feet wet. You are enjoying a long walk with the water tickling your toes. Then a wave hits. It knocks you off your feet and pins you to the sand. The wave rolls out to sea again, but for the moment the fear of drowning hits you with a vengeance. You pick yourself up and begin to walk again.

There are certainly *waves* in the grieving process. The catalyst for the emotions that come may be a special place you enjoyed together, a song on the radio or a certain smell that triggers your memory. To me, the smell of popcorn and cigarette smoke reminds me of football. One whiff and suddenly I am back waiting on the bench at Martin Field in my hometown, praying that I do not have to go into the game.

The perfume they wore or the smell of a hospital can bring back memories, both good and bad. Your response catches you off guard, because you thought you were over the hard part.

You apologize to people for becoming emotional for apparently no reason. You have to regain your composure and then carry on with your day.

I testified at a custody hearing in Bartlesville not long ago. I'm not sure what triggered it, but on the way home to Edmond I began to cry uncontrollably. I started remembering special moments in Jennie's life and began to miss her terribly. My tears dried by the time I got home, but for those two hours, I could not wipe them away fast enough.

I do not believe most people are mean enough to intentionally inflict heartache on someone who is grieving, but a story or a comment can set off a wave as well. Bonnie and I were sitting at a Christmas banquet in Frankenmuth, Michigan shortly after we moved to Flint. The pastor who was in charge of the program gave a very detailed illustration that involved a child dying of cancer. I am sure the man got the illustration from a book, because he showed no emotions when he told the story. The illustration just went well with his presentation. He never knew it, but it felt like he was stabbing us to death. Our emotions were still raw from Jennie's treatment.

I remember checking Jennie into the hospital in Wichita. Jennie was taken up to a room while I gave the information for her admittance. The woman who was checking Jennie in asked if Jennie had a pastor. I said, "Yes, I am her pastor."

When the woman realized what floor Jennie was being admitted to, she said, "Cancer—it is such an awful disease. It seems everyone dies from it. I especially hate it when children die from it."

Then she asked if I knew the name of the parents. I said, "Her mother's name is Bonnie. And I am the father. My name is Randy." The woman could not apologize enough. She would never have hurt me on purpose, but cancer was not personal to her. She would never have spoken those words if she knew my relationship with Jennie first.

I wish I could promise that there will come a time when the waves no longer roll in, but those moments will come. There will be good and bad days. It is hard to accept, but waves are a normal part of the grieving process. I am noticing that the waves are less and less frequently caused by bad memories.

The Bridge of Brokenness

THE WORD PICTURE for this bridge is *limping*. My two examples are greatly exaggerated, but hopefully they will make my point. For those in my generation, focus on the character of Chester on the old *Gunsmoke* television program. For those who are younger, think about Dr. Gregory House of the program *House*. The one thing these two men have in common is that they both limp. Granted, their limp is so noticeable that you cannot miss it, but imagine a person with a less obvious limp. You may not notice it at first, but if you watch carefully there is a little pain with each step.

As I searched for books to read that would help in the healing process, I kept coming across the phrase "New Normal." I read two books by the same author. The second book was entitled, *A New Normal*. The author's son had not died, but was sentenced to prison for life. The first book was helpful in explaining the pain of losing her son, but when I read the second book, I could not find any "normalizing" going on in her life. Years later, she was still fighting to get him out of prison (I would do that, too). She poured her energy and her resources into changing her son's circumstances. But this never convinced me that her life was normal in any way.

I know what counselors are talking about when they use that phrase, but I struggle with accepting it as a reasonable expectation in the grieving process. My life is certainly *new* in many ways. I have moved to a new city with new surroundings. I have to drive four miles to a grocery store instead of stopping in on the way home. Whatever happens, I will be in a new work environment. I agree with the *new* part of the phrase.

However, I do not think my life will ever be *normal* again! My family and I will make adjustments to go on with our life, but my definition of "normal" will always include Jennie. I have a friend who lost his first wife, a sister-in-law, a set of twins and his second wife (from complications from giving birth). How long would it take his life to "normalize" from all those losses? He will adjust to his new circumstances, but it will always be with a limp. If you watch his life carefully, you will see that there is a little pain with each step he takes.

I know this may be a harder phrase to say, but for me the phrase "functionally broken" better describes what I am expecting for the rest of my life. When Jennie died, several chambers in my heart died with her. As much as I would want it, I will never return to that earlier life. There will always be an emptiness that her absence brings. I would have to admit that new chambers opened as well. I feel things more deeply than I have ever felt in my life.

I am able to *function*. I can still do my job. I can talk to people about my beloved Yankees or the weather. I am able to laugh at a good story or joke. If you did not know me well, you may not even see the tears that well-up every so often. You may not notice the break in my voice when something reminds me of my baby girl. As a pastor, I am especially good at putting on my "game face." I have learned to intentionally hide my feelings.

However, I will always have a limp in my step. I am becoming okay with that. It would be unrealistic to think that someone I loved so deeply will not cross my mind every day. I will not deny that I am broken! For me at least, to deny that I am a broken vessel is much harder than just admitting it. As badly as it hurts, God's most effective servants are the broken ones. If you read the Apostle Paul's testimony of the things he suffered for Christ, it makes the *thorn in the flesh* pale in comparison.

When I taught Pastoral Care to those preparing for a life in ministry, the first subject I addressed was the importance of having a *Pastor's Heart*. I would show the DVD of *The Preacher's Wife*. You can see how hardened the Pastor has become. He has tried to act like everything is okay. You can also see a moment when his heart breaks again. It's a great movie.

Until God breaks the heart of His minister, the measure of "success" will be completely distorted. Just like in the corporate world, there are *ladders* in the church. We measure success by *How Many?* and *How Much?* For over thirty years, I filled out an annual report of the church to the General Church. Except for two very short lines, everything was statistics. The task was to describe in ten words or less how the church was doing spiritually. It was easy to write, "Best Year Ever!"

I am sure I am the only one, but the reports caused me to exaggerate how good things were going. It is especially easy to do when you go off percentages in a small church. If you *grew* by one person, it was a 2% gain! Imagine what happened when a family of four started attending? It caused jealousy in me for the "Big Church Pastors." My ego wanted to win the competition. It even became a competition to take home the prize whether it was a certificate, a plaque or a small set of plastic airplane wings like they give children when they fly!

This may sound strange, but I never want to be unbroken. When I am, I get focused on what "I can do." I try too hard and then exhaust my energy and resources. I focus on my *performance* rather than *God's grace*. I always feel like a failure, because someone is ahead of me no matter what I do. Our brokenness keeps us useable for God. Do I like that fact? Absolutely not! But I realize that God does His best work when I am surrendered to Him.

The Apostle Paul testified to that fact when he wrote II Corinthians 4:7-12. Listen to his words:

> But we have this treasure in jars of clay to show that this all-surpassing power is from God and not from us. We are hard pressed on every side, but not crushed; perplexed, but not in despair; persecuted, but not abandoned; struck down, but not destroyed. We always carry around in our body the death of Jesus, so that the life of Jesus may also be revealed in our body. For we who are alive are always being given over to death for Jesus' sake, so that his life may be revealed in our mortal body. So then, death is at work in us, but life is at work in you.

It is an amazing truth that God's love is not based on what we do, but on His desire to be with us! We do not earn God's love any more than our children earn ours. Do you remember when your child began to walk? Bonnie and I were in a Sunday School Board meeting the night Jennie let go of the chair and walked to the wall. Needless to say, Board meeting was dismissed. That picture is still burned into my memory.

Last month, my great-nephew Cayden began walking. I knew he was ready. I even bragged to my niece Mindy that I could teach him to walk in two days. I found something that Cayden wanted bad enough to take a risk. He took one step, then two. When I saw him this week, he was walking anywhere he wanted to go with that shaky walk that one-year-olds have. By the time this book is published, he will have walking, and maybe talking, down to a fine art.

Do you know how many times he has fallen? More than he has walked! Every time he falls, we pick him up and help him try it again. When he walks across the room without falling, we applaud! "Yeah, Baby Cay!" Do you know why? Because we love him so much that we see past the falls to the potential.

I was forty-three years old when I finally realized that Christ offers us a relationship, not a religion. I realized that "God loves me because He loves me." What we must do is *receive* and *accept* His love. He will enable us to walk with Him by holding our hand. If you are grieving, know that God is not a million miles away. He is walking with you every step of the way. Even when you cannot feel Him, He is there. When you cry, He cries as well! When no one else understands your pain, God does!

I do not believe that God has promised us that we will find a place where all hurt is gone. Not on earth, at least! He does not want us to deny our feelings. God just wants to limp with us!

Appendix

Shock and Awe

SHOCK IS AN amazing gift from God. It enables a person to handle unimaginable tasks which normally they would be incapable of doing. I heard of a man who lifted a full-size car off of a person who was pinned by the car. With his adrenalin at an amazing level, he became Superman for long enough to save the person's life.

When you talk to someone right after they lost a loved one, they may seem just fine. Along with their tears, they may tell a funny story about the person's life or say things like, "I'm fine! I'm just glad that Mom is not in any more pain." This person *is not* fine! They are in shock! They may seem fine at the funeral, but realize that the shock will wear off. That is when the grieving person needs support the most.

I have never been in such awe of a person who was in shock than I was of Bonnie right after Jennie died. During the next seven days, Bonnie was . . . well, she was Bonnie! She was a person of great strength and poise. She had an assignment to fulfill. She was going to plan the best celebration service ever. I do not mean she didn't cry, but in the midst of her tears she took on the tough assignment of planning the funeral events.

Although I had initiated a conversation with Stumpf Funeral Home, Bonnie thought Walker-Brown had a better lay-out to host a gathering of our family and friends. She called Steve Walker, a great funeral director and friend. Bonnie said later, "I bet Steve is scared to even look my direction." It would not have mattered who it was, Bonnie would have told them the same thing: "I do not want to see you or the hearse anywhere near the grave site or at the funeral service!" Bonnie did not like the presence of Funeral Directors at funerals. It was too depressing. Steve and Melvin were both very respectful of Bonnie's request.

I do not know how far Steve had to walk to get to the cemetery itself, but we never saw the hearse.

When we went into Walker-Brown to pick out the casket and make other final arrangements, I thought I noticed Steve trying not to make eye contact with Bonnie. That was a wise move. It was nothing personal; Bonnie just knew that if she had to say good-bye to Jennie, it was going to be a celebration like no one had ever seen before. Fortunately, the day of the graveside service, the sun was out and the skies were partly cloudy. If they had not been, I think Bonnie would have been having a personal conversation with God.

Because Jennie had lost so much hair from the chemo she had taken, Bonnie had already ordered a wig and had it shaped and cut by her favorite hairstylist. The dress was picked out along with the jewelry. The flowers were ordered. People who would be involved in the Celebration Service were contacted so the Celebration Folder could be prepared. The Mother of one of her cancer kids was going to tell how much Jennie impacted her son's life. Beth Boyce was singing "His Eye is on The Sparrow." Beth Bidle was going to read a portion of the book *The Worried Little Sparrow*, which she had read to Jennie when Jennie began to worry. McKenzie Jenner, who had made Jennie smile in the hospital by quoting Psalm 23, was going to recite it in Jennie's honor. Bonnie amazed me in the way she took care of every detail!

Our good friends, Kristen and Spence Wilson, stepped in to make phone calls and any arrangements we needed to make. They also filtered our calls and let people know when it was good to call and when it was not so good. I can still remember Kristen's first visit to our home during this time. Kristen and Spence are both psychologists and counselors. Kristen was very sensitive to how emotionally prepared we were for each step.

Since Jennie was going to be buried at Longview Cemetery just outside of Ponca City, Oklahoma, we knew the 75 minute drive would be hard for people to make after the Celebration Service. After talking together, Bonnie laid out a perfect plan. We would have viewing at the church on Monday night for about three hours. The casket would be in the sanctuary with friends there to greet the people. We would visit in the outside foyer. That way, if some people did not want to view the casket, they didn't have to. This was the only timeframe for viewing. It would not be a prolonged process. Bonnie, Robb and I were able to greet family and friends in a relaxed setting.

On Tuesday, June 22, 2010, we held a graveside service at Longview for invited guests and family. We were not trying to exclude anyone, but wanted the graveside service to be an intimate gathering of those who were close to us. I spoke briefly on the subject, "I Should Have Known She was an Angel" using the text of Hebrews 13:2 which reads, "Do not forget to entertain strangers, for by so doing some people have entertained angels without knowing it."

We shared hugs and tears with those who were there. It was a very meaningful time of support and love. Bonnie had planned for all who were invited to the graveside service to come back to Bartlesville for a delicious, full-course meal. Mary Watson, a great friend and cook extraordinaire, prepared a meal fit for a king. It gave us private time to relax before the next day. It was during this time that sweet Rachel shared her dream of Jennie and Gammy with me.

Throughout these difficult hours, Bonnie was able to do things that went far beyond the emotional ability of a Mother who was so close to her daughter. She was focused and determined to make the difficult decisions that needed to be addressed. There would be time for grieving later. The Aftershock would come, but not yet!

God is Good . . . All the Time

I KNOW THIS must sound strange coming from a grieving father, but I enjoyed Jennie's Celebration Service. Yes, I was in shock at the time. I knew the brick wall I would hit later, but that service could not have been a better celebration of my daughter's life. A friend of Spence and Kristen Wilson prepared the most beautiful booklet I have ever seen at a funeral. Bonnie and Robbie had picked out fourteen of their favorite poems Jennie had written. Some of those poems are included in this book.

Robb wrote a poignant obituary to his sister as only Robb could do. I have never gotten compliments on an obituary before, but months after the funeral, people would comment on how beautiful the obituary was. HeeHee (Robb's first attempt to call his sister "Sissy") would have been proud. It was even worth the $600 we were charged by the local newspaper (always get the obituary cost in writing). Robb's obituary is included at the back of the book.

There was a poem written for each member of the immediate family plus works from special occasions. Jennie also delved in to some very difficult times when she struggled with the issues of life. Behind that beautiful smile was often a broken heart. Jennie was a gifted poetess. As I have mentioned earlier, she wrote poems for each of her cancer kids if they died. The poems were read at the child's funeral.

The words to the song "Dancing with the Angels" by Monk and Neagle were printed on the inside cover of the booklet. Instead of being a folder that might get thrown away, each booklet became a fitting gift from Jennie to her family and friends.

I had planned to once again speak about *I Should Have Known She Was an Angel,* but the service was too perfect to be completed with a sermon. The family entered to Steven Chapman's song "With Hope." Bonnie, Robb and I lit a Memorial Candle. Everything that Bonnie had orchestrated went off perfectly. Bonnie had involved so many of our family and friends in the service. I know I am biased, but it was the best-planned funeral I have ever been a part of. I have to believe that Jennie and Jesus were sitting watching the service with a smile on their faces.

After the family processional and the lighting of the Memorial Candle, family members and friends came to share in the service. Baba prayed. Stan read the obituary. Annette Williams sang, "I'll Praise You in the Storm." Our great niece Kaitlin read some *Veggie Tales* notes from Jennie. The remaining Mischief Makers Club members told stories about their "mischiefy" days. Two of Jennie's poems were read, one each by both grandfathers. I loved the moment when Mackenzie Jenner quoted Psalm 23 from memory.

Spence and Kristin Wilson read some of the letters that had been sent by patients and friends. Amy White, Jonah's Mom, shared an explanation of a picture I had seen numerous times. I just missed seeing the "squirt gun." I realized this was a picture from Jennie's "shooting gallery" days at the hospital.

The two Beths in Jennie's life were next. Beth Bidle read from *Worried Little Sparrow.* Beth Boyce sang, "His Eye is on the Sparrow." I was so glad that Beth Bidle didn't sing with Beth Boyce reading. I have heard Beth Bidle sing—she is no Beth Boyce! Love both of you!

Our dear friend Rita Barnes read an original poem entitled "May You Soar with the Angels." It had been nearly two hours of celebration, but for most people it felt like just a few moments.

I had struggled with exactly what I wanted to say at the close of the service. I had not been able to really complete my thoughts. I was going to talk about the letter I had written Jennie at Christmas that would be buried with her, but it just did not seem right. I had five pages of notes, but I had promised Jennie that when she got married, I was going to act and speak as her father, not as a pastor. I never got a chance to fulfill that promise, but I kept my notes in my pocket and spoke very briefly from my heart. I even did my Mickey Mouse impersonation as I talked about loving to make Jennie laugh. I was just going to explain the story, but Bonnie said, "Go ahead—do the Voice!"

I never would have guessed that the service took two hours. As far as I know, nobody left. The service was over, the final prayer had been prayed—but there was one final touch. When the family got up to leave, we left singing "God is Good, All the Time." It was Jennie's favorite choir number. She always ended the song with a loud shout "Woohoo!"

When we got to the end of the song, as a congregation we all shouted "Woohoo!" in unison. Then, Karen Dimond started playing "When They Ring Those Golden Bells." It was a perfect ending to a perfect service. We knew Jennie would be proud! It truly was a celebration of a beautiful life. I remember walking out of the sanctuary with Bonnie and Robb with a smile on my face and a false confidence that I would be okay. After all, if I could speak at my daughter's funeral with confidence, surely I could get back into the pulpit and back into pastoral life.

Everything was going to be okay! Oh yes, I was definitely in shock. When the shock wore off, I was anything but as confident or capable as I felt on June 23, 2010. Shock is a gift from God, but when the shock wears off, God may seem to be a million miles away.

Standing Stone

I NOTED EARLIER that one of my strange quirks is that I *like* cemeteries. Not in some *Halloween 3* kind of way. I just find most cemeteries fascinating. The stories of people's lives are etched on granite in a way you will not find anywhere else. Were they a good father or mother? What was the main focus of their life? Why are some monuments so large while others are almost invisible? The stones are reminders of the life that was lived, good or bad.

My first Sunday at Bartlesville First Nazarene was the Father's Day of 2000. I had planned for some of my new friends to give testimonies about their dad's impact on their life. I based my sermon that Sunday on Joshua 24: 25-27. These verses follow Joshua's covenant renewal speech which includes that powerful verse, As for me and my house, we will serve the Lord. However, I wanted to focus on the *standing stone* that Joshua placed in remembrance of this renewal. I gave out small white rocks to each father who was willing to renew their covenant as a father. It took me forever to wash the dust off those rocks! My text of the verses read:

> *On that day Joshua made a covenant for the people, and there at Shechem he drew up for them decrees and laws. And Joshua recorded these things in the Book of the Law of God. Then he took a large stone and set it up there under the oak near the holy place of the LORD. "See!" he said to all the people. "This stone will be a witness against us. It has heard all the words the LORD has said to us. It will be a witness against you if you are untrue to your God."*

Shortly after that first Sunday, I was introduced to Ray Vander Laan's video series "That the World May Know." He did a section on Standing

Stones. He showed some actual examples. I realized that standing stones are *huge*! I also came to realize that they served as reminders of special events and special people. They make memories become clearer.

When it came time to select Jennie's grave marker, Bonnie, Robb and I met with the representative of Pryse Monuments. We walked around the display area. I knew we wanted an angel on the stone, but every angel they had looked very dark and depressing. That was not Jennie! I also looked at the prices at Pryse and was amazed at how expensive some were. "This is going to be a long day," I thought.

What I didn't know is that Bonnie had been doing some research. She had found a very unique granite stone that was made by sculptors in China. It was a young angel sitting on a park bench with a small bird sitting on the angel's finger. What I loved about it was that the angel looked very happy and lively. To say the least, the price was a "wee bit" higher than I had expected, but it was perfect for Jennie's grave—so unique, so alive.

The representative for Pryse had never seen a stone like it and certainly did not have one in stock. Our family made a unanimous decision to choose the "Angel Stone." It would take longer to get this stone than most, because the Chinese sculptor would start with one large piece of granite and then *chip away anything that was not an angel*! This was more than a piece of granite. It was a piece of art.

When we sent the marker off to be engraved in Ada, Oklahoma, the person who does the engraving called back to Pryse and said she had ordered six of them to be used for her own fam- ily. The woman at Pryse ordered one for display. Even though there may be multiple "works of art" scattered across the country someday, there is one right now that stands in a little country cemetery across the road from Longview Baptist Church outside of Ponca City. Gammy is close by, along with several members of the family. The hillside slopes gently toward a pasture and pond where a herd of cattle graze quietly. Most days, there is a gentle breeze that blows across that cemetery.

When I stand before Jennie's "standing stone," my mind is flooded with so many memories. I love the picture etched in the marble, along with the "stats" about Jennie's life. It is a picture of Jennie and Charlie sitting by a small lake. My emotions vary from tears to laughter, but I will always remember the "angel" that touched my life so greatly! We wanted to engrave one of Jennie's poems on the back, but there wasn't room. Instead, we placed Proverbs 22:11:

*She who loves a pure heart and whose speech is gracious
will have the King for her friend.*

What will your "standing stone" tell about your life? Did you know Jesus? Were you a good parent? Did your life count? When all is said and done, the lives you touched for Christ is all that matters.

Sunflower Seeds are Good
For your Memory

I JUST LOVE those commercials for different kinds of pills that can be taken to improve everything from your love life to your energy level. I do find it hard to believe that a pill can take 30 years off your age or make you look sexy to your wife while you are cleaning the toilet. Call me an unromantic!

Further, I struggle to believe that anyone would buy one of those products after the announcer gets done with all the disclaimers. You know, "If you drink Rev Me Up! every morning, you will have the energy of a 25-year-old . . . Check with your doctor before drinking Rev Me Up! In some cases, Rev Me Up! has been known to cause liver disease, blindness, deafness, inability to walk, diarrhea, vomiting, growths on your nose, leprosy and in a few cases, death! Let me just slow down a little!

That said, I would like to propose to you the newest "cure" for memory loss that I just discovered this summer. Are you ready? Wait for it . . . *sunflowers*! Not sunflower seeds, just sunflowers. You may have noticed that the background picture on the front cover is a sunflower. There is a reason for that.

Shortly after Jennie died, my father-in-law made a picture display in Jennie's memory. It was actually a framed photo of two pictures of Jennie and a sunflower in full bloom. He sent framed copies to family members along with a packet of sunflower seeds. I thought it was a nice idea, but I was not that sure why he chose a sunflower as the symbol.

This spring, Baba planted a few sunflower seeds at our home and challenged every family member to plant sunflowers in Jennie's honor. Now, I have loved sunflower seeds most of my life. I love to taste the saltiness and crack upon the shell to get to that little nut inside. If they are available, I put sunflower seeds on my salad at a restaurant. Still, I did not understand the symbol's significance until I watched the life cycle of our sunflower.

Due to the extremely hot summer we had, our sunflowers had a little trouble getting started. However, one of them grew strong and tall in spite of the heat. It grew right outside our bedroom window. When the right time came, the sunflower developed a beautiful and bright yellow flower. It was gorgeous for several weeks.

I finally figured out that one of the reasons that a sunflower is a perfect symbol for Jennie's life is because sunflowers always keep their "face" on the sun. My dad told me of seeing a whole field of sunflowers with every head turned the same direction. It was very impressive. We even have one sunflower on the side of our house that has grown out and over and then up. It has stretched to the south in order to "see" the sun. I thought I found an exception to the rule, because the flowers on one plant were turned in opposite directions. When the sun came out, I looked again and sure enough they were "facing" the same way.

From the time Jennie accepted Christ into her life, she was a Son follower. There are very few people I have ever met who stayed more focused on Christ than Jennie did. She was extremely sensitive about making sure she was obedient. One of her co-workers told me, "I knew she was a pastor's daughter, because every Wednesday night she had to make sure she was headed for church by 6:30."

I guess Jennie added, "Because if I am late, my Dad will be upset." Just for the record, I never felt that way. As long as she was in the choir when I got done with Bible Study I was fine. I just needed to hear her saying in a loud voice, "Hello, Dad!"

The second reason that a sunflower is a perfect symbol for Jennie's life is that sunflowers always bow their heads as they die. It is as if their death is an act of worship. They bow their heads before the sun realizing that their life is now coming to an end.

The first person I ever watched die was my Grandma Schuneman. Grace Lorena (Lowe) Schuneman was one of the godliest women I have known. She not only was a faithful member of the Caldwell Free Methodist Church, but even saw the newspaper route she worked as an avenue of ministry. Grandma had quite a few physical and emotional problems throughout her life. It was not unusual to find Grandpa Joe hovering over Grandma with a hammer—it was the only way he could "adjust" her neck and put it back in place!

Grandma Grace had a severe stroke two years before she died. She was never really the same after that. As the time grew closer for her passing, the family gathered at the Caldwell Hospital to begin the "sacred waiting." I stepped into the room to be present for this saint to be taken home. Grandma was not awake. She looked like she was peacefully sleeping. In those closing moments of her life, it seemed angels had gathered around her bed to prepare to take her home. God's presence was very close.

The day that Gammy died was even more of a sacred moment, because she was awake for some of those moments. She was able talk with family members and hear them sing a special concert just for her. Before we stepped out of the room, I went to her bedside, told her how she had been a wonderful mother-in-law, and kissed her forehead.

By afternoon, Gammy was beginning to slip into a pre- death coma. Her eyes became the size of a half-dollar when the nurse said, "Morphine." For the rest of the afternoon, her eyes were still with us. She would respond to every comment through her eye motion. Baba and I began to talk about how sacred this moment was . . . more like being in church than a hospital room.

Jennie's death was not that "easy." She suffered and struggled for about four or five weeks in a semi-coma state. Jennie's "worship" came more during the time when she was alert in Jane Phillips and M.D. Anderson. She talked us through the whole process. Like a saint getting ready to rest at last, Jennie seemed to know when it was time to surrender to the reality of her passing. She talked with excitement about being with those who she loved who had gone before. A sunflower symbolized her life.

The third reason that a sunflower is a symbol of Jennie's life is because a sunflower produces much more life after it dies than before. We still have the "head" of the flower in Baba's office. Remember those sunflower seeds that you chew on? At the very heart of the flower there are literally thousands of seeds in perfect symmetry. The harvest will be far greater after the sunflower is gone than during its lifetime. That is Jennie's life!

I have to believe that Jennie is smiling as she sees how her life, her faith and her courage touch so many heart-broken lives. It is now a family tradition that each year we will plant sunflower seeds in Jennie's memory. Now, I know why! My prayer is that I may be a sunflower too! May people remember our lives for how Christ radiated through who we were and who we are.

A Broken Heart Still Beats

BONNIE AND I were riding home together last week. Bonnie asked me, "Will this hurt ever go away?" I had to answer honestly, "No. It will hurt less, but we will always have pain in our heart over Jennie's death."

It still hurts! Shortly after Jennie died, we asked several friends how long the grieving process took for them. The average time frame was three years. That might as well have been an eternity three months after our loss. In two years, I believe we will be able to deal with our loss better than now, but until the day we see Jennie again, there will be a part of our heart that will not heal.

Bonnie's Mom died in November 2007, but there is not a day that goes by that she and her dad do not think of Gammy or deal with the pain of losing her. I have had numerous moments of flashbacks of good times in Jennie's life and the horrible moments of suffering she went through.

As I mentioned earlier in this book, I think it is more realistic to expect that we can reach a level of being functionally broken. Our brokenness will make us useable vessels in God's hands, but there will be days when I am only able to "get by." I had a great aunt named Josephine Helms. Aunt Josephine and her husband Daniel lost a 16-year-old daughter to an infection that developed from a skating accident. Decades later, Charlotte was still a frequent topic of Josephine's conversations. Daniel was a funeral home director and mortician. Josephine dealt with families who had lost a loved one every day. Her brokenness over Charlotte always kept Josephine's heart tender towards those she ministered to. Her work with grieving people was always done with great compassion, because she had been there.

There are things that I can do now that I could not done a year ago. I can make it through some days without crying all day. I am finding new avenues of ministry that I was not equipped to handle before. However, I am prepared to be used for more effective ministry than I have ever known, because I remain broken. That's one reason why I am okay with the fact that I will never be totally healed.

The next time I will call my life *normal* is when I sit at a table in heaven with Jennie, Gammy, Grandpa and Grandma Akin, Grandpa Joe and Grandma Grace Schuneman, and all who have gone before. That was the way I expected life to always be. That revised expectation will impact your life in two ways. First, you will not try to force yourself to heal. Dr. Jerry Porter's advice is helpful to remember when he wrote, "Be gentle with yourself. Allow yourself to heal slowly."

Second, hopefully it will help those of us who are dealing with someone who is grieving. After a pastor lost his son in a shooting accident and his wife to cancer, one of his Board members said, "At my work, we give a person two weeks to get over something like this. Then, it is back to work." That's a harsh and insensitive statement.

One of the doors that God has opened for me at this moment is working with others on a new Grief Recovery material that would be from the present tense perspective, real people sharing their raw emotions during the painful days of loss, when the pain is deep and real. A person who is reflecting back on the death of a loved one from a ten or twelve year perspective has, to some degree, forgotten the intensity of the initial pain. If someone is teaching Grief Recovery who has never lost a loved one, they are like a person who is explaining how to fly an airplane who has never sat down in the pilot's seat. They aren't fit for the job!

I did not realize it at the time, but God has allowed my heart to be broken to prepare me for the next step of my ministry. Out of the pain I have experienced, he has qualified me to follow Him into a totally different type of ministry. My world is full of hurting people. So is yours! From my next-door neighbor who lost his Mom and Dad three weeks apart to the 20 something person who has experienced more pain and loss than most people do in a lifetime.

You will live again, love again, laugh again. You will be productive at work and enjoy it. Your family will smile again. However, your life has been changed forever. Your life has been radically impacted by an event and a person that can never be restored. You and I will have to learn to live with that truth. But in that state of brokenness, God can use you to reach lives you could never have reached before.

I have heard many discussions of whether or not we will have wings in heaven. Will we be like the angels, able to fly from place to place? It really doesn't matter to me. The one thing that is important is that we will be with

Jesus, our Savior. Sin, sickness, fear, heartache and all those painful things we experience on earth will be gone. We will once again be living the life that God intended for us from before the Creation of the World . . . living with Him under His authority.

Besides, I plan to do a lot of walking, anyway. I want one hand in the hand of Jesus and the other in the hand of my daughter, my wife, my son and all my loved ones. I want a lot of hands. And if we do have wings, I will learn to fly after the first thousand years. First I want to enjoy living in a world where they need no sun, because Jesus is the Light. I want to live in the world where everybody present is a sunflower, always facing Jesus, always bowing before His presence and rejoicing in the fruition of the "seeds" that were planted by Christ living through my life.

Oh, I also plan to sit a lot around the Table that God has provided, with my family on all sides, with Jesus right in front of me, able to look into Jennie's baby blue eyes and laughing until we almost cry.

And, yes, continuing my conversations with an angel.

The Epilogue

IT IS ALMOST midnight on September 30, 2011. I will finish the text of this book tomorrow morning and send it off to Adam Robinson for final editing. I suppose if life was fair, I would have a lot to complain about. In so many ways, it has been the lousiest eighteen months of my family's life. Jennie's death, leaving the pastorate, leaving good friends and familiar places has all brought times of tears and loneliness. There is a level of pain that I never thought we could endure. I could easily argue, "I don't deserve this!" My daughter was the most innocent person I have ever known. No one deserved to live more than she did.

The fact is, life isn't fair! Jesus never promised fairness. Instead He said in John 16:33, "I have told you these things that in Me you may have peace. *In this world you will have trouble, but take heart! I have overcome the world!*" What Jesus promised was His presence! I do not take that promise lightly. There are times in life when all we have is Him.

Today has been a good day! Just listen to the good things that have happened.

It was Bonnie's birthday! We went to Deep Fork Grill and had the best sirloin steak you can imagine. My manager friend Lauren not only made all the arrangements, but sent a plate full of every dessert they have. My new friend Heather made an extra effort to cater to our every need. It was a blast.

Eric Thurman, the owner of ET Barbeque, made me—I mean Bonnie—a delicious and warm cherry cobbler that was to die for. Between the desserts and the cobbler, I have to believe I will set an all-time record with my sugar level tonight. Has anyone ever reached the 2,000 point level?

Phillips, Craig and Dean were in concert last night. I got to hear "my boys" sing their hearts out. While they were singing in the second half of the program, God gave me most of the words to Jennie's song. The song will be officially entitled "A Deeper Kind of Grace." I used four tithe envelopes as my scratch pad.

Sandi Patty, Larnelle Harris, Wayne Watson and Heather Bryan were in concert at Crossings Community Church last Sunday night. I got to sit next to John Bond while he listened for the first time to Sandy and Larnelle sing "I've Just Seen Jesus." That's what I'm talking about!

Bonnie, Baba and I got to sip coffee on the back porch this morning and watch the Morning Glories grow.

I got to do my Mickey Mouse voice for my sister. It made her laugh!

We sat out on the back porch tonight and enjoyed the beautiful evening breeze.

My friend Mackenzie Jenner got encouraging news from the doctor.

I enjoyed a great meal at Olive Garden with great friends. Ann Lundberg paid. Thanks, Ann!

Shelley Breen from Point of Grace sent me a text message saying that she was taking a song title I gave her to Tony Woods. Tony and I go back to his "Revelation of a Sailor" days. (Okay, that's a joke. I haven't met him . . . yet!)

Today, my wife laughed! That is always a good day!

Robb and I did not talk politics! That also is always a good day!

Baba ate more than Peanut Butter! That is an unbelievably good day!

The Yankees made it to the post-season again!

OU is on its way to a Bowl Game.

In addition to all these blessings, my toughest decision all summer has been what t-shirt to wear. (I am trying to collect those "Tour Date" t-shirts from heavy metal bands). I have my own "man cave." I have made some new friends. God has provided for our needs. Best of all, I have awakened every morning, checked my email to see if where I am going to work is ready to hire me, then spent the rest of the day being Wind-blown! *"Lord, where are we going today?"* In so many ways, I have never enjoyed life more . . . except when Jennie was with us.

Our conversations are not over today. In fact, they are just beginning. As I now have entered my second year of grief, I realize how great the need is for those who have known the pain of losing a loved one to talk to each other. Only those who have walked down this road can truly understand and feel the emotions of this unique grieving process. I hope you'll take a minute to visit our website, at www.JennieShoe.com, and leave a message.

This book is also not finished today. When my sermons went too long, I always excused my length by quoting from John 16:12 where Jesus said, "I have much more to say to you, more than you can now bear." Check the website for additional— free—chapters, because I am still on the journey. I'm on the journey with you! Through Christ, we are going to make it!

Jennie's Obituary

by *Robb Schuneman*

JENNIE DAWN SCHUNEMAN, a beloved daughter and sister, a registered nurse, a passionate lover of God, and a compassionate lover of people, passed away the afternoon of June 17, 2010 at the age of 32, following a 10-week battle with her second bout of cancer.

When she was 4 years old, Jennie was diagnosed with ovarian cancer. Over the next two years of treatment neither her beautiful smile, nor her young but dynamic faith in God would waiver. When she was miraculously healed, her recovery leaving doctors puzzled and her family rejoicing, God began to use her story, her faith, and her brilliant smile to heal countless others, inside and out.

She crafted and perfected that smile growing up in Flint, Michigan, and through endless summer days on her Grand- parents' farms. Trips to be with her beloved Oklahoma family in Red Rock and Medford for Christmases, summers, spring breaks, and whenever else possible were the highlight of her year. Uncles and aunts were more like second parents, cousins more like siblings, and grandparents more like best friends who sometimes cooked you incredible meals or taught you how life worked.

As she reached high school, Jen began to feel the first heart tugs of a calling that would define her life. She saw a unique opportunity to use the miracle of her healing to bring comfort and hope to others. It was then that she decided to go into the medical field, and to work specifically in pediatric oncology.

This mission led Jennie to Spring Arbor College in Spring Arbor Michigan, where she graduated with a Bachelor of Arts in Biology in 2000. During these years, her calling was confirmed through several amazing summers spent as a counselor with Special Days Camps, a program that provides a traditional camp experience for children living with cancer. It was at Spring Arbor, also, that Jennie fully bloomed, gaining the confidence to share the dancing, singing, fun-making girl her family knew so well with the rest of the world, and developing some of her closest friendships along the way.

It was the combination of this "anything to get a laugh" personality, combined with Jennie's heart for children stricken with cancer, that led her, in 2003, to complete a second degree, a Bachelor of Science in Nursing from the University of Central Oklahoma. Shortly after, she achieved Certified Pediatric Oncology Nurse (CPON) status. It was her stated desire to pursue nursing over other forms of medicine in order to be able to develop closer relationships with her patients and their families, to be able to hug them when they were hurting, and to lead the parades when they had reason to rejoice.

And she did exactly that and so much more while working at OU Children's Hospital in Oklahoma City, St. Francis Children's Hospital in Tulsa, and most recently, Jane Phillips Medical Center in Bartlesville.

She brought this same enthusiasm and sweet spirit to Bartlesville First Church of the Nazarene, where she was an active member, a caretaker of "her little angels" in the nursery, and continued to spread her contagious smile to all whom she worshipped with. Singing came from Jennie's heart, whether it was in the choir, leading worship on the Praise Team, or actively being involved in drama, specifically Promise of Hope. Her small group led her to close friendships, and developed her confidence to share her personal relationship with Jesus Christ with others.

Jennie was also accomplished as a pianist and was a talented poet. Her Mother was her first piano teacher, beginning at the age of five, but certainly was not the last. She continued her keyboard training throughout college, and always found her heart expressed through the white and black keys.

Jennie began writing at a very young age, winning many local competitions. Family events, both joyous and sad, were celebrated and witnessed by Jennie's hand through very meaningful and expressive poems. A few of Jennie's works have been published into a booklet, and will be distributed to family and friends at Wednesday's Celebration Service.

Jennie is survived by her parents, Dr. Randy and Bonnie Schuneman, of Bartlesville, brother, Robb Schuneman, of Bartlesville, grandparents, Harold Mullins, of Bartlesville (formerly of Red Rock, OK), and Don and Millie Schuneman of Medford, Oklahoma. Aunts and Uncles include

Jenarold and Larry Jones of Edmond, Stan and Vicky Mullins of Perry, Mike and Becky Mullins of Shawnee, and Judy and Wes Meisner of Lincoln, Nebraska. Cousins held a special place in Jennie's life, comparing more to brothers and sisters. They include Becky Slothower of Edmond, Dan Jones of Denver, Jamie Cessna of Wichita, Cindy Keathly of Edmond, Mindy Cook of Edmond, Natalie Stanford of Ft. Lauderdale, Nathan Mullins of Perry, Cami Mullins of Houston, Matt Mullins of Shawnee, Jonathan Meisner of Bethany, and Mendy Cummins of Bethany. But the latest generation of little ones were the apple of her eye: Kaitlin, Kenzie, Mariah and Rachel Slothower of Edmond, Michael Jones of Edmond, Daniel and Shantal Jones of Denver, Henry Stanford of Ft. Lauderdale, Hannah and Wyatt Mullins of Perry, Anabelle Keathly of Edmond, and four-week-old "Baby Cayden Cook" of Edmond. Jen leaves aching hearts in a host of loving friends and her church family. Jennie was hugged tightly and smothered with kisses by her Gammy, Jennie Bernice Mullins, who preceded her in death.

Jennie's family and friends are invited to a Come and Go visitation and viewing on Monday, June 21st, from 5 p.m. to 8 p.m. in the main foyer of Bartlesville First Church of the Nazarene. A private family burial will be held on Tuesday, June 22nd, at the Longwood Cemetery in Ponca City, Oklahoma.

A glorious celebration of Jennie's life will be held Wednesday, June 23rd, at 1 p.m. at Bartlesville First Church of the Nazarene, where Jennie's Dad serves as Lead Pastor. Jennie will also lie in state at Walker Brown Funeral Home on Sunday, June 20, from 12 to 6 p.m. Walker Brown Funeral Home has been entrusted with the earthly arrangements for our precious Jennie - God has taken care of the rest - He has her back!

Acknowledgments

I could not have told this story right now if it had not been for some very special people who have walked with me through this process. Some are new friends while I have known others all of my life. Let me take a moment to thank them.

As a first-time author, I had no idea how to publish a book. When I made an informational call to WestBow Press, I was fortunate to reach Jenniffer Mollet (pronounced *mow-lay* in France). In the midst of a conversation about the business procedures of publishing, I remember the moment I began to talk about why I was writing this book. As I began to talk about my daughter's story, Jenniffer not only heard my tears, but wept with me. I remember praying together at the end of the conversation for God's guidance and blessings. Jenniffer and I have never met (although we are Facebook friends), but she has been a cheerleader for this writing endeavor from the very beginning.

This book is seamless. Each chapter can stand on its own. The book was not written chronologically. Each chapter was written as God laid it on my heart. To try to weave a book together while it is being written would be a nightmare for most editors, but my son Robb introduced me via email, phone and text messages to a college acquaintance, Adam Robinson. Adam is a genius! I was able to send chapters as I wrote them and have Adam organize them for me. It has been a true blessing to talk to Adam on a daily basis. Most importantly, Adam has come to understand my passion for telling Jennie's story. His advice has been invaluable. Adam and I have never met (although too we are Facebook friends), but he has become an important part of the molding process that God is taking me through.

My parents, Don and Millie Schuneman have known me all my life and believe in me anyway! They have supported me with their prayers and helped underwrite some of the financial costs of this book. They also served on my "first-time readers" team, taking turns reading the original manuscript in order to give me feedback.

My father-in-law, Harold Mullins was the first person to read the manuscript. He also introduced me to the image of the sunflower which serves as the underlining word picture for Jennie's life. Through his wisdom, Harold taught me how the sunflower symbolizes the goal of life, to produce more seeds after we are gone than when we were alive.

Dave Clark was the first person I called when I found out that Jennie was going to die. What a beautiful Foreword he has provided here! Dave, thanks for being there when I needed you.

I have never amounted to much, but I have great friends! Thanks to Dan Dean, Sandi Patty, Shelley Breen, Michael Christensen and Leonard Sweet for taking time to read chapters from the book and give their blessings. Each blurb is a work of art!

Special thanks to Laura Andrus, whose friendship meant the world to Jennie. Congratulations on your first child. Thanks also to Kim Betts who made Jennie's last days of nursing her best!

Dr. Randy Schuneman is a minister at large who has pastored and taught as an elder in the Church of the Nazarene for 33 years. He has pastored in Wichita, Kansas, Flint, Michigan and Bartlesville, Oklahoma. He has also served as an adjunct professor at Oklahoma Wesleyan University, Southern Nazarene University and Spring Arbor University.

Dr. Schuneman is a graduate of Drew University, Nazarene Theological Seminary and Southern Nazarene University.

Randy is a die-hard Yankees and Celtics fan who loves baseball memorabilia, lighthouses and a good story.

He and his wife Bonnie now reside in Edmond, Oklahoma. Their son Robb resides in Edmond as well.

Made in the USA
Lexington, KY
16 June 2012